Why Are You Hiding, God?

Why Are You Hiding, God?

D. L. SEEKER

RESOURCE *Publications* · Eugene, Oregon

WHY ARE YOU HIDING, GOD?

Copyright © 2021 D. L. Seeker. All rights reserved. Except for brief quotations in critical publications or reviews, no part of this book may be reproduced in any manner without prior written permission from the publisher. Write: Permissions, Wipf and Stock Publishers, 199 W. 8th Ave., Suite 3, Eugene, OR 97401.

Resource Publications
An Imprint of Wipf and Stock Publishers
199 W. 8th Ave., Suite 3
Eugene, OR 97401

www.wipfandstock.com

PAPERBACK ISBN: 978-1-6667-0775-5
HARDCOVER ISBN: 978-1-6667-0776-2
EBOOK ISBN: 978-1-6667-0777-9

All verses quoted in this book are from the King James Version of the Bible.

Any added words in parentheses are from me.

I draw some things from my two previous self-published books which are *Imploding into God's Love* and *Jesus Keeps Me This Side of Crazy*.

The names have been changed in this book, but it is true as much as I am able to make it true.

06/08/21

This book is dedicated to God and all his children.

Contents

Chapter One: Cosmic Hide-and-Seek ... 1
Chapter Two: Angels versus Demons ... 59
Chapter Three: Love Implosion ... 84
Chapter Four: Hell versus Heaven ... 103
Chapter Five: Triangular Wisdom ... 139
Chapter Six: Human Consciousness Is Human Spirit and Soul ... 150

Chapter One

Cosmic Hide-and-Seek

CONFUSION

> Driving along life's superhighway, I see neon signs flashing by.
> Where do I turn, oh where do I turn?
> "Fear not," God says. "My Spirit and book will guide you."
> What is wrong and what is right?
> Confusion leaps out of the night.
> Where shall I turn, oh where shall I turn?
> "Fear not," Jesus says. "My Spirit and book will guide you."

Dear God,
Where are you? Why are you hiding? Where are you hiding? Why have you made yourself invisible to the five senses you gave me to explore this material world with? How am I supposed to find and connect to you like this? You want me to put my faith in you and if you are even a little bit as wonderful as I perceive that you are, there is no one I would rather put my faith in and have a relationship with than you, but it is often hard for me to find you. I am often not sure that I am connecting and communicating with you the way you want me to or the way I want to. Sometimes I'm not sure if I am communicating with you, the real God, or some fantasy version of you

that my mind has made up, or if I go back and forth between the real you and the fantasy you. If you are everywhere like the Bible says you are, and you put clues in the world for people to find where you are hiding so they can become your children and develop a closer friendship as your children, how do I find you? I know you say you can be found by faith, but why would you set the world up to find you by faith when that makes it so difficult to discern the real you from the fantasy you? Then even when we find you and become your children, it takes more than a lifetime to find out what is or is not really true about you and your ways. I almost feel that to connect with you I have to let you develop a sixth sense in me that I don't know how to activate or use. I am going to try my best, using this sixth sense, to guess where you are hiding.

Isaiah 45:15: "Verily thou art a God that hidest thyself, O God of Israel, the Saviour."

Hebrews 11:6: "But without faith it is impossible to please him; for he that cometh to God must believe that he is, and that he is a rewarder of them that diligently seek him."

I think you are hiding in the Bible. Why are you hiding in a book written by prophets that you inspired? People have been born into the timeline of earth before your Bible was even started, while it's books were being written, or even after they were completed. I believe the Bible is the only completely true book about you, completely accurate in the original manuscripts that you inspired men to write over a time period of hundreds of years. It is historically and scientifically accurate. The prophecies of things that you tell will happen before they happen are accurate. The true stories of actual people that choose to live, or to not live, their lives by faith in you are accurate. You told these men that were inspired by your Spirit how you began the earth and how you will end it. If you are the true God that creates all life and sustains everything—except evil, which you allow for now—then I can only assume that you are able to keep a book about yourself true through all of history. The truths you teach us about in the Bible often focus on people who lived their lives while having a growing relationship with you. You jumble our human timeline as your prophets talk about the present and future and past, while only being present in their present because you created our timeline and you come in and out of our human timeline but you think and live out of time. Since you live in and out of time, the thoughts you transfer to us are above us. Your prophets also talk about the Messiah's comings and goings in the Bible out of order on our human timeline, and this can get confusing as well. Also, I get that most of the stories in the Bible are about people who were believers in you and were trying to live their earthly lives with you, but they all lived before many of the inventions and much of the education we live with today. These things have only appeared on the earth timeline in about the last 200 years. Before that, people cooked over fires, raised animals and grew plants for their food, had more social interaction with humans and animals for survival. They didn't have cell phones, computers, cars, planes, social media, refrigerators, ovens, plumbing, electricity, television, internet, or other things that we Americans take for granted today. Sometimes it is hard for me to relate in this technological age I live in. However, I see that your essence never changes and the fact that all humans are made in your image never changes.

Isaiah 46:9-10: "Remember the former things of old; for I am God, and there is none else; I am God, and there is none like me, declaring the end from the beginning, and from ancient times the things that are not yet done, saying, 'My counsel shall stand, and I will do all my pleasure.'"

Daniel 12:4: "But thou, O Daniel, shut up the words, and seal the book, even to the time of the end; many shall run to and fro, and knowledge shall be increased."

I guess humans are born hiding from you. From what I learn about you from this book, the Bible, it seems you have always been calling to people to become your children and communicate with you in the hidden garden of their heart, or their spirit-soul. When you first made people, you interacted with them in friendship in bodily form in a beautiful garden. You, the Father, Son, and Holy Spirit, probably came to talk to Adam and Eve in a human form that Jesus projected. Adam and Eve and you had sweet fellowship together in the garden. If they had never let evil in, things could have continued in perfect harmony like this forever. Animals and people just ate plants and everyone was happy and were friends. Then, when they listened to the fallen angel, Lucifer, who had shape-shifted into the form of a talking snake, and they chose to let evil enter your world, you kicked them out of the garden and became invisible to people in the material realm, and they could only find you in the invisible garden of their hearts if they invited you in by becoming your child. Adam and Eve became your children and some of their children became your children and some of their children did not become your children. Ever since the first human was born lost to you, every human has been born lost to you, and you have sought to find each one of us. When we become your child, then we are found by you and we are not lost anymore, so I guess humans are hiding from you as well. Some of us want you to find us and you want all of us to want to be found by you and for us to seek a closer and closer relationship with you. I guess you will continue to play this cosmic game of hide-and-seek with humans until the last human that will ever be born is born.

Luke 19:10: "For the Son of man is come to seek and to save that which was lost."

You knew humans would listen to a fallen angel to let evil enter their world, and you planned to redeem them before you even made them. Evil's terminal destruction had already entered the fallen angels, and then it entered the world and everyone and everything created in the world, and only you knew what had to be done to overcome evil, and only you had the power to do it, and you did it and are doing it.

Titus 1:2: "In hope of eternal life, which God, that cannot lie, promised before the world began."

Genesis 3:3–6: "But the fruit of the tree which is in the midst of the garden, God hath said, 'Ye shall not eat of it, neither shall ye touch it, lest ye die.' And the serpent said unto the woman, 'Ye shall not surely die; for God doth know that in the day ye eat thereof, then your eyes shall be opened, and ye shall be as gods, knowing good and evil.' And when the woman saw that the tree was good for food, and that it was pleasant to the eyes, and a tree to be desired to make one wise, she took of the fruit thereof, and did eat, and gave also unto her husband with her and he did eat."

I think you are hiding in the way you set this earth up to appear self-sustaining, despite it being sustained by you. Is our life journey more than a game of hide-and-seek or some other game? Is human life a game, or one big test, or a series of tests, or a continuous school? Or are we born into some kind of war, or is it some kind of combination? What is all of this really all about? Humans just enter the world one day and we can't see the beginning and we can't see beyond death and everyone is saying something different about what life is really all about. I want to find out from you what life is all about, but I have to keep finding where you are hiding so that I can hear a little more communication from you before you hide from me again and I have to find you again.

I think you are also hiding in the secret thoughts you are transmitting to each of your children. Once humans are your children, I guess you speak in our thoughts with your Spirit all the time, not just when we read the Bible. It is often hard for me to discern what you are getting at as you personalize your thoughts into mine using anything and everything. You lead step by step, sending messages that grip my mind as I try to find your will for me in earth's confusing, boring, scary, and beautiful moments. I want to learn to identify and obey the voice of your Spirit in my thoughts to a greater and greater extent as I live out my life. I am trying not to block your voice to me, though I know I do this at various times. Connecting and communicating with you are completely different than connecting and communicating with anyone else in the universe. Prayer is talking and listening to you. It seems sort of like mental telepathy. You are the one true God and no one else is like you. You are so completely one of a kind that I guess any relationship you form with those whom you have made will be completely unique, which can be confusing. I guess you only made angels and people with a sentient spirit-soul, and so those are the only creatures that can form a true love relationship with you. I guess you are in our very consciousness and there is no more intimate place than that.

Ephesians 4:30: "And grieve not the holy Spirit of God, whereby ye are sealed unto the day of redemption."

I think you are hiding in the love and blessings that you give to everyone and everything, but that you especially give to your people and angel children. Angels and humans are the only ones that you created with a spirit so that they can connect to you. You want to love and be loved because your very essence is love. Love always seeks the good of the one that is loved. Love also seeks to give good happiness and pleasure to the one that is loved.

I think you are also hiding in the earthly battle between good and evil. True love is freely given and received, so, in forming sentient beings, you had to allow the possibility for the door to evil to be opened, knowing what it would cost you to close it. People can never be good enough to rid themselves of the evil they are born in and with, and only your power can save any human who receives that gift that you decided to provide before the world began. You had to allow free will in angels and people to choose to go the way of evil or to choose to bind to you in love, to eventually be free from evil because their free will wants you more than they want anyone or anything, including evil. Evil, or sin, is doing or thinking anything that you would not want done or thought, so of course you never made evil, you created and continue to sustain everything and everyone except evil. Though you allow evil to be sustained in a way for a time, it has its consequences within your boundaries while you are allowing it on this earth to let your angel and human children battle it with you. You probably do this so that we will learn to hate evil as much as you do as we become touched experientially by it. You don't hate any angels or people whether they are your children or not, but you hate evil and you hate any evil that touches them because evil is so hurtful to anyone it touches and its pleasures always turn into pain. You are in the process of overcoming evil with good in such a way that all your angel and human sentient children will see why when you decide to completely close the door to evil. You are allowing evil to invade the world right now and angels and people are learning about it experientially.

I think you are hiding in the spirit-soul connection that you have had and have and will have with all your human children while they are on earth. You never gave us humans a choice when to enter this material world, but you say you give us a choice whether we want to enter your invisible world by telling you that we want you to adopt us into your family, by coming to you in repentance and faith, which includes many things like eventually being free from all evil. I used the free will you gave me to choose to let you link your Spirit to mine as I came to you in repentance and faith, and your friendship is the most important thing in the universe to me, my Father-God. You are not like anyone else and your love is electric and life-giving. You entered into my essence with your love and brought me into your family as your adopted daughter, which brought me into your kingdom, since you are the true king of all the universe. Since this is all in the realm of outward invisibility in this material world for this time, people that don't know you can think I'm crazy. I guess one of the places that you are hiding is inside me and all your other human believer children. I guess one of your hiding places is the human heart.

John 14:22–23: "Judas saith unto him, not Iscariot, Lord, How is it that thou wilt manifest thyself unto us, and not unto the world? Jesus answered and said unto him, If a man love me, he will keep my words; and my Father will love him, and we will come unto him, and make our abode with him."

First Corinthians 1:18: "For the preaching of the cross is to them that perish foolishness; but unto us which are saved it is the power of God."

I think you are hiding in the groups of people you formed to shine a light to the world so they can see and connect to the one true God, like family units that show your ways, like the children of Adam and Eve that chose to become your children, like Noah and his family, like the Hebrew nation, and like the church. It isn't always easy to be in a relationship with you, now that you are my Father and I am your daughter, as I try to figure out who you are and who I am, and who you are to me and who I am to you, and who all our other family members are in relationship with us, with you always as our center. You created my soul—which I guess is my mind, will, conscience, emotions, and consciousness—to dwell inside my material body. My spirit—which I guess is the invisible part of me that can make a connection with you—seems to be attached to my soul, which also dwells in my body. I was born slated for my spirit, soul, and body to eventually die in the time set for them to be gone. My body will still die but you gave eternal life to my spirit and soul when I became your child and someday you will put them in a new eternal body as well. My spirit-soul was dead until you synergistically connected me to your Spirit and made it come alive. I guess when my spirit came alive, I became born again and this caused me to become a whole new person. Now I am able to hear your voice, even though every day I struggle to figure out which one is your voice in all the thoughts that come to me. Then when I think that I am hearing your voice in my thoughts, I struggle to understand the meaning of what you are communicating to me.

John 10:27–28: "My sheep hear my voice, and I know them, and they follow me; and I give unto them eternal life; and they shall never perish, neither shall any man pluck them out of my hand."

Colossians 1:12–18, "Giving thanks unto the Father, which hath made us meet to be partakers of the inheritance of the saints in light; who hath delivered us from the power of darkness, and hath translated us into the kingdom of his dear Son; in whom we have redemption through his blood, even the forgiveness of sins; who is the image of the invisible God, the firstborn of every creature; for by him were all things created, that are in heaven, and that are in earth, visible and invisible, whether they be thrones, or dominions, or principalities, or powers; all things were created by him and for him; and he is before all things, and by him all things consist. And he is the head of the body, the church; who is the beginning, the firstborn from the dead; that in all things he might have the preeminence."

I think you often call the spirit and soul part of me by different names in the Bible, like my heart, soul, or spirit, but sometimes one term means all of them or just one of them. Your Bible is hard to decipher and I continually call on your Spirit to help me understand what meaning you are trying to give me. My joining with you may not be easy and the friendship may not always be easy, but joining with you was the only way I could find the ultimate true love I had longed for. You say faith is a requirement for a human to join and grow with you on this earth, from the time of Adam and Eve until the last person is born. Only you and the angels know how long this earth has been here and only you know when it will end. At this point you will contain and burn away all evil from your universe. People try to act like they know when the world was created, but how could they, since no human alive today was here when you created the earth? You only give clues to your earthly timeline. The way humans interpret these clues are very much influenced by their core beliefs.

I think you also seem to be hiding in the faith that humans give you. You set things up for us to reach you by faith partly by being materially invisible to us, but when my soul and spirit leave my body I will be completely with you and I will no longer need faith. I will be a happy, sentient, floating soul-spirit, living joyfully with you, and someday at your rapture you will give me a new immortal body. My soul-spirit will probably have the capability to project whatever bodily form I want to shape-shift into at this point.

Matthew 17:1–3: "And after six days Jesus taketh Peter, James, and John his brother, and bringeth them up into an high mountain apart, and was transfigured before them; and his face did shine as the sun, and his raiment was white as the light. And, behold, there appeared unto them Moses and Elias talking with him."

I will always need faith to interact with you here and my faith will increase, step by step, as I grow with you, though I will never be one hundred percent sure of anything until I am in heaven with you, my dear Father, brother, friend, mentor, counselor, and love of my life. Even though you keep yourself in the realm of faith here on earth, I know enough about you to know that putting my growing relationship with you first is the thing I want most in my life and the thing you want most for me. I don't completely understand why you keep hiding, but I will never stop seeking you as you are seeking me, because no one else is worth finding like you are. You transform and heal all my internal mess and I walk around with this transformed life, trying to shine your light in the darkness so that other people will see that you not only are hiding in faith, hope, and love, but that you are ultimate hope and love. The synergistic love relationship doesn't transform me into you, but it transforms me into the person you had in mind for me to become when you created me, the person I really want to be inside, the person I can only be and become more of when I am in a close, synergistic relationship with you. Everything you do is so different because everything you do is about pure love.

Romans 1:17: "For therein is the righteousness of God revealed from faith to faith; as it is written, 'The just shall live by faith.'"

Hebrews 11:6: But without faith it is impossible to please him; for he that cometh to God must believe that he is and that he is a rewarder of them that diligently seek him."

First Corinthians 13:12–13: "For now we see through a glass, darkly; but then face to face; now I know in part; but then shall I know even as also I am known. And now abideth faith, hope, charity (love), these three, but the greatest of these is charity (love)."

Second Corinthians 5:6–8: "Therefore we are always confident, knowing that, whilst we are at home in the body, we are absent from the Lord; for we walk by faith, not by sight; we are confident, I say, and willing rather to be absent from the body, and to be present with the Lord."

Matthew 5:16: "Let your light so shine before men, that they may see your good works, and glorify your Father which is in heaven."

Second Corinthians 5:17: "Therefore, if any man be in Christ, he is a new creature; old things are passed away; behold all things are become new."

Romans 8:9: "But ye are not in the flesh, but in the Spirit, if so be that the Spirit of God dwell in you. Now if any man have not the Spirit of Christ, he is none of his."

Romans 8:14: "For as many as are led by the Spirit of God, they are the sons of God."

I think you are hiding in hope. There is hope for each person who is not your child that they will become your child. There is hope that each of your children will enter heaven with you when their spirit-soul is released by their bodily death. There is hope for a beautiful inward transformation for each of your children as they spend time with you. You don't live in people who don't invite you in, but you still love them and bless them and hope they will invite you in. Your original design was not for people or angels to live disconnected from you, but people are born disconnected now and they have to choose to become your child and then after that they have to choose how deeply they are going to connect with you, step by step, as they live out their life story on earth. Angels that chose to disconnect from you and humans that never connect to you will burn away and be gone in hell because they are not connected to your immortal Spirit, and your love causes you to grieve for these lost to you. After their physical death, their soul-spirit will eventually be burned away at some point like the people would burn the chaff away after sifting out the wheat.

Matthew 3:12: "Whose fan is in his hand, and he will thoroughly purge his floor, and gather his wheat into the garner; but he will burn up the chaff with unquenchable fire."

You did not create the angels with any genetic link. If you had not created hell, then you would not be fighting evil; if you were not fighting evil, then you would become evil; and then there would truly be no hope for the universe if the one true God turned evil instead of good.

Matthew 5:45: "That ye may be the children of your Father which is in heaven; for he maketh his sun to rise on the evil and on the good and sendeth rain on the just and on the unjust."

Second Corinthians 5:15: "And that he died for all, that they which live should not henceforth live unto themselves, but unto him which died for them, and rose again."

Second Corinthians 5:20–21: "Now then, we are ambassadors for Christ, as though God did beseech you by us; we pray you in Christ's stead, be ye reconciled to God. For he hath made him to be sin for us, who knew no sin; that we might be made the righteousness of God in him."

John 14:23: "Jesus answered and said unto him, 'If a man love me, he will keep my words; and my Father will love him, and we will come unto him, and make our abode with him.'"

Romans 6:23: "For the wages of sin is death; but the gift of God is eternal life through Jesus Christ our Lord."

I think you are hiding in the secret miracles you give your children, and as we talk and listen to you. Much of your healing, communication, and help are only given by you when we choose to pray for some reason. Your Spirit helps us pray.

This is my personal life journal of my prayers to you and the communication I perceive back from you. Only your Bible is without error in the original manuscripts. I know priests and translators, when copying it for future generations, have been very careful to try to remain true to the original wording. I know I don't get everything right in this my journal book, but hopefully I am getting enough right in reflecting our relationship to show how beyond wonderful being in a relationship with you really is. I can hardly believe that you, God, would actually want a close friendship with me. Sometimes I feel so messed up that I don't even want to hang out with myself. Your love shows me how to love you, others, and myself. Your love helps me keep becoming the person I really want to be, the person you created me to be. Your love makes me feel wild and free, and your love helps me be steadily becomebhu the person I really want to be. I can see following you in a loving friendship is the most important thing in the world. You are the greatest treasure in the universe.

Matthew 22:36–40: "'Master, which is the great commandment in the law?' Jesus said unto him, 'Thou shalt love the Lord thy God with all thy heart, and with all thy soul, and with all thy mind. This is the first and great commandment. And the second is like unto it, "Thou shalt love thy neighbour as thyself." On these two commandments hang all the law and the prophets.'"

Romans 5:8: "But God commendeth his love toward us, in that, while we were yet sinners, Christ died for us."

I've changed the names of the people in my book since it isn't their fault that their lives got mixed in with the life of a writer somehow. My book is as true as I can make it as I live my life with you, knowing that it is impossible for me to be completely accurate since I popped in this world at a time you decided, and I wasn't here when you made the world, and I will leave before you end it. I have limited knowledge. You decided to give me knowledge from your Spirit for the time and place you created me in, and for your good purposes.

People wanted the knowledge of evil as well as good, and we are getting it. I find myself wanting that knowledge as well, and then wishing I didn't. I am finding out experientially why you hate evil so much. It has its own charming pull at the beginning, but then it always hurts everyone involved in a more painful way than could ever have been imagined. It often puts us into bondage and addictive traps that only you can free us from. I have knowledge of good and evil and I try not to get the two mixed up in this deceptive world. Sometimes evil starts out very exciting and fun, but then it always hurts so bad in the end. Sometimes good starts out so hard, but it always ends up so beautiful in the end. You designed me a certain way, using my mother and father, but I can only willingly find and do your individual purposes for me when I am closely connected to you.

You created the first human from soil. You created his wife from his rib. Their children grew up and got married and from then on, you created all humans using their mother and father. So all humans are genetically linked to one another and can trace their ancestry back to Adam and Eve. Angels do not share a genetic link. Because of the genetic link that you placed in all humans, Jesus was able to turn himself into a God-man and live a life free from the infection of evil, so that when he willingly gave up his body to be killed, he became the sacrifice and the cure to free those who wanted to receive his gift from the ultimate curse of evil. Evil seems to be passed to all humans genetically through their father, so when the Holy Spirit popped baby Jesus into Mary's womb, he only used the genetics of Jesus' mother to form his humanity. That is why Jesus was born of a virgin. Jesus still could have chosen to open the door to evil just like Adam and Eve did, but he was loving and strong enough to not open it so that he could become the perfect human sacrifice to all the humans he shared a genetic link with, which is all humans.

The fallen angels who were created as adults in your heavenly home knew that there would be no redemption for them as they followed Lucifer/Satan out of heaven and disconnected themselves from you. They have no genetic link. Now they spend their time on earth using their powers to keep people from making that connection with you that your redemption made possible. If they can't keep people from joining you, then they try to keep them from growing in relationship with you. They don't want any angels or people to be your connected friends. They want angels and people to live disconnected from you the way that they do.

I don't see why Satan thinks he or anyone can take your place as God in a sentient being's life. You are the only life not created, and it would be impossible for you to create another god because that god would be created and therefore would not be you: the true, eternal, uncreated God. You know everything and you created time to interact with us because you live in and outside of time. You are everywhere and fill the universe, and even though you hide, you are always aware of everyone and everything. You alone are immortal. You were always here and you will always be here. So you did not create me to be God, you created me to become a daughter of you, God. In acknowledging that you are the only true master of everyone and everything, I can be happy and find inward freedom in being who you made me to be. I surrender more and more to you as I come to know and trust your character more and more.

I think you are hiding in time. If creation scientists are right and this earth is only almost 6,000 years old and your Messiah entered it 4,000 some years into its existence, creating BC and AD, then you put me here around 2,000 years after your Messiah became a God-man. He lived, died, and resurrected his human life to pay for the sins of all his human brothers and sisters that wanted to receive his perfect payment. Humans are genetically linked to Jesus and that is what he had to do to save us. Maybe the earth will go on until it hits 7,000 years, and then your Messiah will rule the earth bodily for 1,000 years as a Sabbath rest for the earth, reflecting the seven days you used for earth's creation. At this time more people will choose to become your children than those who don't choose to become your children. Then when these last 1,000 years are over, you will destroy the earth and sky with fire and make a new earth and sky without any evil. Any sentient beings that chose evil over you will be burned away and forever gone after they have served the time and punishment in hell that your final judgment hands down to them. I don't know if any of these times are right or not and I can't really know until I'm with you in heaven, so I need to let it go. I guess time is one of the other places that you are hiding in.

Malachi 3:16: "Then they that feared the Lord spake often one to another; and the Lord hearkened, and heard it, and a book of remembrance was written before him for them that feared the Lord, and that thought upon his name."

Psalms 139:16: "Thine eyes did see my substance, yet being unperfect; and in thy book all my members were written, which in continuance were fashioned, when as yet there was none of them."

Matthew 16:25: "For whosoever will save his life shall lose it; and whosoever will lose his life for my sake shall find it."

2 Peter 3:7–10: "But the heavens and the earth, which are now, by the same word are kept in store, reserved unto fire against the day of judgment and perdition of ungodly men. But, beloved, be not ignorant of this one thing, that one day is with the Lord as a thousand years, and a thousand years as one day. The Lord is not slack concerning his promise, as some men count slackness; but is longsuffering to usward, not willing that any should perish, but that all should come to repentance. But the day of the Lord will come as a thief in the night; in the which the heavens shall pass away with a great noise, and the elements shall melt with fervent heat, the earth also and the works that are therein shall be burned up."

Sometimes I kiss my Bible as a token expression of my love for you. Having your Spirit personalize the words in your Bible for each of your children is a unique way to grow the intimate love relationship you have with each of your children. I know the devil likes to copy you a lot and he and his fallen angels try to get people to write books that they can hide in. Please keep the evil spirits out of my head and out of this prayer journal book I am writing because fallen angels like to confuse all of us humans about who you are. They hate you for some reason, and don't want you to have any true friends. I want to be your true friend and I am sorry whenever I let them trick me away from closeness with you. They seem to be able to talk in my thoughts when I let them. Sometimes I really can't believe that you, the most awesome being in the universe, actually want to be my best friend. I mess up so much. I'm so glad that you have a forgiving heart. I am so glad that you can use your love powers to transform me day by day, eternally, into who I really want to be as your friend. You help me forgive myself and others with your forgiving power.

I think you also seem to be hiding in our human identity. You made all humans in your image, but they do not become real until they allow you to synergistically mix with them when they come to you in repentance and faith and let your Spirit link to their spirit. Being made in your image enables this to happen, but it can only happen by the free choice of each human. I used to argue with all my Christian brothers and sisters about who you are and what your Bible, rules, and plans are really all about. I didn't understand that you are the ultimate love relationship all humans long for, and not merely a friendship. You never intended us to be perfect Christian robots that all look the same when we reach that elusive place of being mature Christians. I thought this was true for a good portion of my life and I became very angry inside, trying to conform myself and everyone else into what I thought this perfect Christian robot should look and act like. Now, I realize that you are above comprehension and you have such an individual relationship with each of us that it is only together that we can do all the different jobs that are needed in each plan and purpose you have. Our individual identity comes from you and we all will shine your light in different ways. The more I surrender to you, the more I seem to become the person I have always really wanted to be. Surrendering to you seems to make me less of a robot and more free, which seems to work in the opposite way when I surrender my essence to anyone or anything else other than you, even if it is my own self. You place clues along our life journey to help us discover who you are, who we are, and who others are, and who we are all together. I guess you are also hiding in the purposes we find you have for each of us.

Genesis 1:27: "So God created man in his own image, in the image of God created he him; male and female created he them."

I think you are hiding in heaven. You are the Trinity, God. You are three persons in one. You have many names throughout time, but I mostly know you as the Father, Son (Jesus), and Holy Spirit. You created people on a different planet from your heaven and with less knowledge and power than the angels possessed. I think you did this partly so angels and people could get a firsthand experiential understanding of why you hate evil and want it gone as we fight for your side. You knew how emotionally hard it would be to finally extinguish evil from your universe once it was let in by angels, and then by people, without becoming evil yourself. You knew what you had to do, and so you did it and are doing it. Jesus is our Messiah. He is the one true superhero for the human race and the universe. This is thrilling and confusing at the same time. Adam opened the door of evil so that every human is born lost to you in sin, and only Jesus can shut the door to the eventual destruction that evil brings with it. People could become your children even before Jesus died because your promise that you would conquer evil through your Messiah was and is enough. I so appreciate you doing what you had to do so that I could be your forever child.

Genesis 3:15: "And I will put enmity between thee and the woman, and between thy seed and her seed; it shall bruise thy head, and thou shalt bruise his heel."

Honestly, probably any human you put on this earth first would have opened the door to evil just like Adam and Eve did. I probably would have done the same thing. We just had to experience evil to see why you hate evil so much, and now we see. We could have lived forever on earth if we hadn't let evil's terminal infection in, but as soon as we let evil in, every part of our human selves became slated for death, and everything else that you created on the earth also became cursed by evil and slated for death. We see our bodies eventually die, but we can't see beyond death. We can't see what you do with our soul and spirit after this. Believers have faith that their soul and spirit will fly into your loving arms forever and escape any death and destruction by your grace, but we can't see this happen while we are on earth because you are also hiding in heaven.

Titus 3:9: "But avoid foolish questions, and genealogies, and contentions, and strivings about the law; for they are unprofitable and vain."

Matthew 28:19: "Go ye therefore, and teach all nations, baptizing them in the name of the Father, and of the Son, and of the Holy Ghost."

Romans 5:18: "Therefore as by the offence of one judgment came upon all men to condemnation; even so by the righteousness of one the free gift came upon all men unto justification of life."

Luke 19:10: For the Son of man is come to seek and to save that which was lost."

John 14:3: "And if I go and prepare a place for you. I will come again, and receive you unto myself; that where I am, there ye may be also."

I think you are hiding in your creation and in the functionality of your scientific and moral laws. All of the material realm seems to be a pointer toward the spiritual realm. We came out from the water of our mother's womb for our first birth, and then your Spirit calls through the soul of every human to let you connect your Spirit to their spirit. When we choose to become your adopted child through repentance and faith, you synergistically link your Spirit to our spirit for our second birth as our spirit comes alive in you, and then we enter your kingdom as your forever children. This all sounds a bit like science fiction, but then life itself is beyond comprehension and we have to decide to trust you or not, with however much information you give us on our faith journey.

As I read your Bible I see some of the things you are saying are just for a certain person or group of people in a certain time and place, and then some of the words that you speak are for all people, for all time. The stories and cultures of people change over time. It is amazing how your Bible can speak to one person about their particular situation in history, and then decades or centuries later, that same message will be exactly what an entirely different person needs.

John 14:17: "Even the Spirit of truth; whom the world cannot receive, because it seeth him not, neither knoweth him; but ye know him; for he dwelleth with you, and shall be in you."

People have been becoming your children since the beginning of time, even before your Messiah came and people knew his name was and is Jesus, and before you finished inspiring your Bible. People showed their repentance to you and faith in you and your ability to forgive their sin by offering animal sacrifices even before they completely understood about what you would have to do through your Messiah to make this all possible. Since you never lie, people could come to you before the Messiah came because you said he would come, and he came and did what he needed to do. There is nothing we had to do to become your child except come to you in repentance and faith, and once we are your child, there is nothing we can do to become disconnected from being your child. As soon as a human becomes your child, you link your Spirit to their spirit forever with a spiritual link that cannot be broken.

John 3:5-7: "Jesus answered, 'Verily, verily, I say unto thee, Except a man be born of water and of the Spirit, he cannot enter into the kingdom of God. That which is born of the flesh is flesh; and that which is born of the Spirit is spirit. Marvel not that I said unto thee, "Ye must be born again."'"

Hebrews 11:3-4: "Through faith we understand that the worlds were framed by the word of God, so that things which are seen were not made of things which do appear. By faith Abel offered unto God a more excellent sacrifice than Cain, by which he obtained witness that he was righteous, God testifying of his gifts; and by it he being dead yet speaketh."

Dear Christie,
Why are you teaching me and preaching to me? You do realize I am God, right?

Dear God,
I'm sorry. Since you speak in our thoughts right now and ask us to speak some of the things we learn from you out to other people for right now, I am just trying to sort it all through.

Dear Christie,
I realize that it can be a bit confusing to develop a personal relationship with me while you are on this earth, but I am longing to help you through everything, and that includes growing more intimate with me. I love you. I am waiting for you each time you open your eyes and ears to see and hear me with your heart, and for you to find the next clue to find me in the places I am hiding, and follow my guidance and loving friendship to draw closer and closer into my love. I am your greatest reward. I am more than an imaginary God projection, or a philosophical or religious concept. I am the

heartbeat of the universe. I am your best friend. No one will ever love you the way I do. I totally understand you even though your understanding of me comes in baby steps on earth. No one will ever know or love you the way I do. I set this world up for you to have a relationship with me and to figure our relationship out, and I may appear to be hiding but I am always with you. I want you to constantly seek me out. I am here and there and everywhere, and I am caring about you through all the joys, doubts, confusions, blessings, and troubles that make up your earthly life. Trust me to bring you through your earth-bound journey, through all its confusing ups and downs, as we grow closer and you gain more of my eternal God perspective. Even though I never send evil to anyone or anything, I allow it to enter at times as it follows its natural course of entrance because I know I can use it to teach my children things about good, evil, and me in ways that they could never learn about such things without trusting me and seeing my power overcoming evil with my good personally. Trust me when evil touches your life and when you fight its pull. I never give evil, but I am allowing it to have some of its consequences on the earth.

Never stop seeking me and finding me in all of my hiding places until you are with me in our home in heaven where there will be no more hiding. I am hiding in miracles. The laws of science and the laws of good and evil have their interplay now, but I am still working my miracles, even though they often appear as coincidences. I am hiding in miracles right now as I constantly overcome evil with good. People wanted to have the knowledge of evil, and now they have it. I created everything, except evil. I am stronger than evil and only I know how to deal with its destructive force. I am doing this at great personal cost because I love humans enough to fight evil for and with them experientially in such a way that at the end of earth time this knowledge of good and evil will make all the angels and humans who choose me willingly never want to open the door to evil again, once it is finally and completely shut forever.

Yes, the spiritual is a mystery for humans to continuously solve, but once someone joins my family I give them the ability to detect and solve clues to find more and more truth. My Spirit gives them spiritual receptors that enable them to talk and listen to me. Animals and plants never ask themselves who made them and why they are here on the earth, and who made the world they live in. They never ask themselves if there is a Creator. They never ask themselves that if there is a Creator, would there be a possibility to have a relationship with that Creator. The fact that only humans out of all the earth creatures ask themselves these questions is a big clue that humans have something no other earth creatures have, which is a spirit linked to their soul.

There are many clues that only humans are made in my image with a spirit that is meant to link with me. One big clue to the human soul-spirit is the fact that animals and plants do not have the moral conscience and the consciousness that humans do. A human can never be complete or truly alive until they choose to link their spirit to mine. My Spirit calls to each human spirit to join me. I call into the soul of each human for them to let me link my Spirit to theirs. Animals may have a soul, but there are clues that they are lacking a spirit. God, marriage, murder, and the ability to understand scientific and moral laws, and many other things that are in all human consciousness on some level, are not found in animals and plants. Fallen angel spirits may try to deceive others into thinking that they are the spirits of animals, plants, dead people, gods, spirit guides, aliens, false philosophies and religions, and anyone and anything else they can fake to trick people out of friendship with me, but these spirits are just the spirit-souls of fallen angels. These fallen angels may have more knowledge and powers than people have, but their spirits are dead to me.

I need to hide to fight evil as long as I allow evil to be on the earth. Evil is in all the earth and I am in the process of destroying that infection with my love and justice, so if a human dies too young or too disabled to make the free will choice to join me, I bring them home to me because they never had the chance to make their own choice to answer the call of my Spirit that calls into the soul of every human to allow me to connect their spirit with mine. This is something only I can do and no human can be free enough from evil to do it for themselves. Those humans who choose not to allow me to connect their spirit to my Spirit in repentance and faith never become truly real in my love and they will eventually completely burn away and be gone, along with the fallen angels.

I am hiding in my creation and in the functionality of the material world. While Jesus lived physically on the earth, he was constantly pointing out that the visible is a pointer to the invisible in many ways. Your spirit, alive, enables us to communicate with each other while you live on the earth. My voice becomes clearer to you each time you confess to, surrender to, and obey me no matter how many times you have sinned or missed me before. Everyone and everything in the world, sky, and heaven will eventually pass away, except those spirits connected to me.

Genesis 15:1: "After these things the word of the Lord came unto Abram in a vision, saying, 'Fear not, Abram; I am thy shield, and thy exceeding great reward.'"

Isaiah 45:15: "Verily thou art a God that hidest thyself, O God of Israel, the Saviour."

Romans 1:20: "For the invisible things of him from the creation of the world are clearly seen, being understood by the things that are made, even his eternal power and Godhead; so that they are without excuse."

First Corinthians 2:11–12, 16: "For what man knoweth the things of a man, save the spirit of man which is in him? Even so the things of God knoweth no man, but the Spirit of God. Now we have received, not the spirit of the world, but the spirit which is of God; that we might know the things that are freely given to us of God. For who hath known the mind of the Lord, that he may instruct him? But we have the mind of Christ."

First Timothy 2:4: "Who will have all men to be saved, and to come unto the knowledge of the truth?"

Isaiah 45:22: "Look unto me, and be ye saved, all the ends of the earth; for I am God, and there is none else."

Second Samuel 12:22–23: "And he said, 'While the child was yet alive, I fasted and wept; for I said, "Who can tell whether God will be gracious to me, that the child may live?" But now he is dead, wherefore should I fast? Can I bring him back again? I shall go to him but he shall not return to me.'"

Ephesians 2:8–9: "For by grace are ye saved through faith; and that not of yourselves; it is the gift of God; not of works, lest any man should boast."

First Corinthians 1:18: "For the preaching of the cross is to them that perish foolishness, but unto us which are saved it is the power of God."

Hebrews 12:27–29: "And this word, yet once more signifieth the removing of those things that are shaken, as of things that are made, that those things which cannot be shaken may remain. Wherefore we receiving a kingdom which cannot be moved, let us have grace, whereby we may serve God acceptably with reverence and godly fear; for our God is a consuming fire."

Dear Christie,

Ever since Adam and Eve, it has been very easy for any human to become my child. All they had to do was come to me in their thoughts, in repentance and faith, with as little or as much information as they had in the time and place they lived in, and I came to them and connected my Spirit to their spirit and they became forever mine and I became forever theirs.

Romans 3:23: "For all have sinned, and come short of the glory of God."

Dear Christie,

Fallen angels and unbelieving people can have a type of life apart from me, but it never becomes real or immortal because it is not connected to me and it will eventually burn away like chaff and be gone. I did not create anyone immortal, no matter what earthly philosophers say. There is no where in the Bible that I say anyone is immortal, except me, and I only let my angel and people children share my immortality when they are linked to me, the only immortal one. Unbelieving people and fallen angels may even manage to stay out of a lot of evil's traps and find some fulfillment in life by following the good moral conscience I created them with, but they are still choosing to live their lives unjoined to me and they are not connected to ultimate truth and love because that can only be found in me. I never designed angels or humans to live unjoined to me, and because they want to choose their own way, apart from me, they can never be truly real. Even though I love everyone, I am who I am.

Exodus 3:14: "And God said unto Moses, 'I am that I am'; and he said, 'Thus shalt thou say unto the children of Israel, "I am hath sent me unto you."'"

Satan does not want anyone to share my love or acknowledge who I am. Satan influences fallen angels and unbelieving people to live a life unlinked to me by influencing people to take anyone or anything for their lord and master except me, even their own selves. They forget that even though I made this free will possible, they would not even be able to function within any framework, linked to me or not, if I did not give and sustain life. My blessings fall to a certain extent on everyone, whether they are my children or not. Fallen angels and unbelieving humans can find a functioning life that they choose to find, but they will someday be gone, just as all earthly life without an alive spirit will be gone, and they will never find ultimate love and fulfillment because this can only be found in a relationship with me. If anyone was truly able to kill me, the universe and everything and everyone in it would cease to exist and become just like the blank screen you have when you shut off your computer.

John 3:16: "For God so loved the world, that he gave his only begotten Son, that whosoever believeth in him should not perish, but have everlasting life."

Matthew 3:12: "Whose fan is in his hand, and he will thoroughly purge his floor, and gather his wheat into the garner; but he will burn up the chaff with unquenchable fire."

Matthew 5:44–45: "But I say unto you, love your enemies, bless them that curse you, do good to them that hate you, and pray for them which despitefully use you, and persecute you. That ye may be the children of your Father which is in heaven; for he maketh his sun to rise on the evil and on the good, and sendeth rain on the just and the unjust."

Dear Christie,

When sin entered the world, it's evil terminal infection caused everyone and everything formed in this world to be cursed and slated for destruction. Only spirits joined with me will escape this destruction. I am the greatest love, and anyone connected to me is connected to the greatest love. Human love, as well as many other things about human existence, can point toward finding a connection with me, but no one can know ultimate love that is great enough to make spirits real without this connection to me. I alone am immortal.

1 John 4:8–9: "He that loveth not knoweth not God; for God is love. In this was manifested the love of God toward us, because that God sent his only begotten Son into the world, that we might live through him."

1 Timothy 6:16: "Who only hath immortality, dwelling in the light which no man can approach unto, whom no man hath seen, nor can see; to whom be honour and power everlasting. Amen."

Dear God,

Do you think it is entirely fair that you ask believing humans to serve an invisible God with an invisible spirit and fight invisible enemies that have a lot more power than us right now, with invisible weapons, while we live in a material world with a material body that has five senses in it? I think the way you communicate with us here on earth through faith has the possibility of leaving us open to a lot of fantasies and deceptions. Sometimes it is very hard to separate fantasy from reality. Also, many of your truths come to light over much time.

Ephesians 6:10–18: "Finally, my brethren, be strong in the Lord, and in the power of his might. Put on the whole armour of God, that ye may be able to stand against the wiles of the devil. For we wrestle not against flesh and blood, but against principalities, against powers, against the rulers of the darkness of this world, against spiritual wickedness in high places. Wherefore take unto you the whole armour of God, that ye may be able to withstand in the evil day, and having done all, to stand. Stand therefore, having your loins girt about with truth, and having on the breastplate of righteousness; And your feet shod with the preparation of the gospel of peace; above all, taking the shield of faith, wherewith ye shall be able to quench all the fiery darts of the wicked. And take the helmet of salvation, and the sword of the Spirit, which is the word of God; praying always with all prayer and supplication jin the Spirit, and watching thereunto with all perseverance and supplications for all saints."

Dear Christie,
What does your heart tell you?

Dear God,

I guess you are hiding in our hearts, in a garden place of sweet interaction with us, your children, where we worship and talk with you and you talk with us. It is a place where you heal, help, and teach us. In this place you also play with us and talk with us and listen to us. I have to admit that following even the best choices offered by fallen angels or others, never gives me inside what only you give me. Your amazing friendship love keeps me coming back to seek where you are hiding, again and again, to try to get closer to you. I've gone both ways and I know your way is always best, even though it doesn't always look the best at first glance. If evil spirits can't keep us from choosing to be adopted by you, they never stop trying to take our minds away from you in any way they can. Their pull never stops, and giving into their influence feels like being taken over by evil aliens, which I guess it sort of is. Even though you never disown me and I am always connected to your Spirit, I can still block your influence over me in this life and open doors for evil spirits to be my friends and confidants. And I know from personal experience what terrible traps they can lead me into that often seem very pleasant at first. I also know that you have the power to get me out of any of those traps if I just completely surrender to you. Sin hurts others and myself and everyone it touches, I guess that is partly why you hate it so much.

Most of the miracles that you often give to your believing children can often be written off as coincidence, I guess to keep everything in the realm of faith. There are many truth mysteries that we humans will not solve on this earth, though we will keep solving more until things clear up a lot more when we come to you. Then there will be mysteries to solve for eternity, but it won't be so frustrating because you will be right there with us, face to face. I know you are God and I know you always know best, even though I am constantly leaving this place of surrender to you and fellowship with you and then struggling to get back to the place of sweet fellowship with you inside myself in the secret garden of my heart. Adam and Eve let evil in and you kicked them and all people out of the garden, where we could fellowship with you face to face. You and the garden turned invisible. You make a way for any human who becomes your child to come to this fellowship garden with you internally until we can fully live there again with you in the garden of heaven. I wish I would stay in the garden with you instead of allowing confusion, fear, anger, trials, hardships, deceptions, and having to live with evil pull me away again. I know I never stop being your child, but I am so sad when I don't feel close to you and so happy when I do feel close to you. When people look at a Christian, they see Christians going through problems just like everyone else, but they may not see you always helping us internally through everything in the secret garden of love that you share with us in our heart.

Galatians 5:22–23: "But the fruit of the Spirit is love, joy, peace, longsuffering, gentleness, goodness, faith, meekness, temperance: against such there is no law."

You give blessings of materials, health, fame, friendship, power, and worldly success of some kind to some of your children and do not give them to others. It is hard to figure why any people, Christians or not, go through the hardships and experience the success that they do on this earth because sometimes it has to do with the causes and effects of what they do and don't do, and sometimes it has nothing to do with them at all. Every person has their own life journey and story, and only you can completely understand why. All fear is gone when we come to you in the garden that you are always hiding in, waiting for us to come and be with you, where you give us your love, wisdom, and strength for each step of our journey.

Galatians 5:22–23: "But the fruit of the Spirit is love, joy, peace, longsuffering, gentleness, goodness, faith, meekness, temperance: against such there is no law."

Second Timothy 1:7: "For God hath not given us the spirit of fear; but of power, and of love, and of a sound mind."

In the world people live in today, the world seems to say, whether a person is a believer or not, that only those people who excel above other people are real and all the other people really don't count. You have to be a superstar in singing, fame, politics, art, beauty, intellect, preaching, authorship, sports, newscasting, drama, partying, music, differing technology, popularity, acting, science, wealth, inventions, or anything else to give the world the impression that we are not invisible, especially the more media, social or otherwise, consumes us. There is nothing wrong with people excelling, using the strengths and talents you gave them, if that is in your plan for them. There is something wrong with thinking we become real when our dreams are accomplished instead of knowing we only become real when we allow you to link your Spirit to our spirit. Following you should always be the dream of each of your children wherever that may lead them on their earth journey. Our success is finding out what your will is for us for each minute and being happy to do it because of our love and trust in you, even if the road that you lead other people on looks so much more inviting than the road that you are leading us on. This means we are willing to do your will with our lives for the purposes you have for us individually, whether that involves fame, comfort, popularity, fortune, money, or not. This means that we are not jealous or despising of another human walking on whatever life journey they are walking on. We shouldn't be jealous of the life plan you have for someone else, but we should be happy with whatever the life plan is that you have for us, because we have you, and that is enough.

1 John 2:16–17: "For all that is in the world, the lust of the flesh, and the lust of the eyes, and the pride of life, is not of the Father but is of the world. And the world passeth away, and the lust thereof; but he that doeth the will of God abideth forever."

Matthew 6:24: "No man can serve two masters; for either he will hate the one and love the other; or else he will hold to the one, and despise the other. Ye cannot serve God and mammon (money)."

Our connection with you is partly about letting the love we share with you shine through our lives, no matter what our circumstances, to help other people find the true God in the darkness of evil. You are love to me, so why do I keep allowing myself to get pulled into the deception of finding my identity apart from you in fame, money, popularity, comfort, or power? I see the quick thrill of evil leads to a place away from intimacy with you, which always ends in hurt, unhappiness, and despair, so why am I still dreaming dreams of being able to find myself in my will instead of yours?

I guess Satan, who also seems to be able to invade our thoughts when we let him, wants us to think we can be happiest following dreams that have nothing to do with our connection to you.

First Corinthians 12:12–13: "For now we see through a glass, darkly; but then face to face; now I know in part; but then shall I know even as also I am known. And now abideth faith, hope, charity (love), these three; but the greatest of these is charity (love).

First Corinthians 12:18: "But now hath God set the members every one of them in the body, as it hath pleased him."

First John 2:16: "For all that is in the world, the lust of the flesh, and the lust of the eyes, and the pride of life, is not of the Father, but is of the world. And the world passeth away, and the lust thereof; but he that doeth the will of God abideth forever."

Isaiah 14:12–14: "How art thou fallen from heaven, O Lucifer, son of the morning! How art thou cut down to the ground, which didst weaken the nations! For thou hast said in thine heart, 'I will ascend into heaven, I will exalt my throne above the stars of God; I will sit also upon the mount of the congregation, in the sides of the north; I will ascend above the clouds; I will be like the most high.'"

Romans 9:20–23: "Nay but, O man, who art thou that repliest against God? Shall the thing formed say to him that formed it, 'Why hast thou made me thus?' Hath not the potter power over the clay, of the same lump to make one vessel unto honour, and another unto dishonour? What if God, willing to shew his wrath, and to make his power known, endured with much longsuffering the vessels of wrath fitted to destruction; and that he might make known the riches of his glory on the vessels of mercy, which he had afore prepared unto glory?"

Dear Christie,
Many people are saying things about me that are completely untrue. They may want money or power or something else besides my working in their life, so they say religious things that have nothing to do with my thoughts, even though they say they are speaking for me. You need to double check everything every person says about me through my Bible and Spirit, and look at the way they live in their family and community to see if they are really following me. I know it is hard to figure things out, but trust me, my love and wisdom are more than enough to help you through your journey here during your time on earth where you just won't understand as much as you want to understand. I come into people and make them mine and I let these people tell others who I am during earth time. Yes, Satan may try to trick others this way, and people may not get everything right this way, and I may reflect out of true believers in different ways depending on what purposes I have for them, but this keeps me in the realm of faith on the earth. Faith is a step-by-step walk as you constantly reach for my hand. You step out with as much guidance as you can perceive I am giving you and only then will I give you the next step and help you grow in our relationship. I am ultimate love, and when you became connected to my love, you received what I long for every human to receive when I chose to create all humans in my image: a loving relationship with me.

Let me help you get unstuck at the place you are in so that you can personally move forward with me. Sometimes you just seem to walk in circles, spinning round and round and not moving forward at all. I didn't give you a spiritual mind for this. The more you give up yourself to anyone or anything except me, even yourself, the more you become a trapped slave. I enable you to become more and more internally free and more the person you really want to be, the person I had in mind for you to become when I created you in my image. Your internal heart is what is most important to me, and what I think should always count most with you. Love invites, it doesn't force. Let me be the dream you dream. Let the desires I have for you be your desires.

Second Peter 3:9: "The Lord is not slack concerning his promise, as some men count slackness; but is longsuffering to usward, not willing that any should perish, but that all should come to repentance."

Philippians 1:6: "Being confident of this very thing, that he which hath begun a good work in you will perform it until the day of Jesus Christ."

First Samuel 16:7: "But the Lord said unto Samuel, 'Look not on his countenance, or on the height of his stature; because I have refused him; for the Lord seeth not as man seeth, for man looketh on the outward appearance, but the Lord looketh on the heart.'"

Psalms 37:4: "Delight thyself also in the Lord; and he shall give thee the desires of thine heart."

Dear Christie,

I want you to be open and honest with me as you seek to grow closer with me in love and understanding, but always be open to my redirection as you travel on your life path, because the glimmer that you perceive may misdirect your steps. I want you to be careful to never think that I am evil, or that I cause any evil. I am always bringing you through evil so that my goodness and wisdom fills more and more of your life. Always remember my character as you go through your earthly tests, even when evil touches you without and pulls at you from within. I am good and I am fighting to overcome evil with good. I am stronger than any evil. I am stronger than anyone or anything. Abraham understood my character when I asked him to go through the test of sacrificing the son that he loved more than anyone, except me. He thought to himself that since I don't condone murder that if he had to sacrafice Isaac that I would immediately raise Isaac from the dead. Then he saw I stopped him before he actually did this and provided a ram for him to sacrifice instead. His test was so all people could see how torn my heart was when I had to allow my only son to be sacrificed on a cross. Abraham's faith through his test of truly believing in my character of love, justice, and goodness, even as he walked through a terrifying path that he didn't understand, let him be the founding father for all believers that would come in the Hebrew nation and the church.

Hebrews 11:17-19: "By faith Abraham, when he was tried, offered up Isaac; and he that had received the promises offered up his only begotten sin, of whom it was said, that in Isaac shall thy seed be called; accounting that God was able to raise him up, even from the dead; from whence also he received him in a figure."

Dear God,

I think it would be a lot easier for me if you would call or text me, or send Jesus down to talk to me, person to person, but I know your faith plan is better for now, even if it often seems quite curious. I guess it would be a little scary and confusing if you talked to me so that my ears heard you instead of my thoughts perceiving your messages because of the way you have things set up for now. Your Bible is often hard for me to understand, especially the King James Version. Who talks like that anymore? Why does it mostly refer to people as men even though it means men, women, boys, and girls? Also, the differing communication you have had with people since evil entered the world is radically different than almost any other communication that we have.

I think the Bible seems to say that there seem to be immaterial portals in our material world that can be opened and closed to commune with you or fallen angels by the choices we humans make. Unfallen angels that are your children are always only redirecting us back to you and your Spirit in wanting us to follow your directions like they always do. I long to be closer to you. Please help me.

John 10:9: "I am the door; by me if any man enter in, he shall be saved, and shall go in and out, and find pasture."

Dear God,

My spiritual receivers and codes seem to be off lately as I try to talk and listen with you here and now.

Isaiah 59:2: "But your iniquities have separated between you and your God, and your sins have hid his face from you, that he will not hear."

Romans 12:21: "Be not overcome of evil, but overcome evil with good."

First Corinthians 13:4–5: "Charity (love) suffereth long, and is kind; charity (love) envieth not; charity (love) vaunteth not itself, is not puffed up, doth not behave itself unseemly, seeketh not her own, is not easily provoked, thinketh no evil."

Proverbs 29:11: "A fool uttereth all his mind; but a wise man keepeth it in till afterwards."

James 1:20: "For the wrath of man worketh not the righteousness of God."

Romans 8:14: "For as many as are led by the Spirit of God, they are the sons of God."

Luke 18:9–14: "And he spake this parable unto certain which trusted in themselves that they were righteous, and despised others; two men went up into the temple to pray; the one a Pharisee, and the other a publican. The Pharisee stood and prayed thus with himself, 'God, I thank thee, that I am not as other men are, extortioners, unjust, adulterers, or even as this publican I fast twice in the week, I give tithes of all that I possess.' And the publican, standing afar off, would not lift up so much as his eyes unto heaven, but smote upon his breast, saying, 'God be merciful to me a sinner.' I tell you, this man went down to his house justified rather than the other;

for every one that exalteth himself shall be abased; and he that humbleth himself shall be exalted."

Second Corinthians 3:5–6: "Not that we are sufficient of ourselves to think anything as of ourselves; but our sufficiency is of God; who also hath made us able ministers of the new testament; not of the letter, but of the spirit; for the letter killeth, but the spirit giveth life."

Dear God,

Why are you always quoting verses to me? I know I am causing a rift in our relationship right now. Yes, I do want to listen to your answers to my questions. I just want to remind you of a few things in case you forgot. I have been your child since I was four. My dad was a minister and my mom helped him with his church ministry a lot as his wife. I was raised in the church and I helped my parents in their church ministry and at home as I was growing up. I have been a teacher in Christian schools for over forty years. I have tried to keep your laws. I have to say that it hasn't always been easy to try to think and do everything in your way, one that people think is more extreme than how things should be thought about or done. On the other hand, sometimes even religious people can really seem to be off their rocker. I've been in church and in the world all my life so I should know. My husband often acts like a baby Christian. I think I try harder with you than most other people do.

Okay, I hear what you are saying to me now. Wow, I guess you are right, I do sound like that one Pharisee guy, don't I? Yes, Father, I would love to have a close relationship with you more than just some religion, even if I have to let go of the pride of living my way instead of yours to do it, even if I have to give up my dreams and take on your dreams for me to do it. Please help me to become unstuck in my own pride and to cease in longing for my own personal heaven on earth instead of greater friendship with you, and draw me closer to walk in your unconventional ways, even if I don't get my own way. I know you always know best and I am miserable when I am not close with you. When I judge others instead of seeing them with your loving and forgiving eyes, I turn those same judging and unforgiving eyes on myself, and I don't have your help to get me out of this unpleasant trap until I give my anger and vengeance to you. Then I become happy that you want to love and transform everyone, even evil people who are mean to me and others. I need to stand up for myself, others, and the truth of your way, and never take revenge no matter how things turn out. I'm not saying what the other person did was right when I forgive, I am just saying that you are trying to overcome evil with good, and only you are righteous enough to decide what punishment each one receives at the final judgment. Please help me find my way back to closeness with you. I will seek you again. I know your hiding places. You want me to find you. Help me.

Romans 12:17–21: "Recompense to no man evil for evil. Provide things honest in the sight of all men. If it be possible, as much as lieth in you, live peaceably with all men. Dearly beloved, avenge not yourselves, but rather give place unto wrath; for it is written, 'Vengeance is mine; I will repay,' saith the Lord. Therefore if thine enemy hunger, feed him; if he thirst, give him drink; for in so doing thou shalt heap coals of fire on his head. Be not overcome of evil, but overcome evil with good."

First Peter 1:12: "Unto whom it was revealed, that not unto themselves, but unto us they did minister the things, which are now reported unto you by them that have preached the gospel unto you with the Holy Ghost sent down from heaven; which things the angels desire to look into."

Romans 5:12: "Wherefore, as by one man sin entered the world, and death by sin; and so death passed upon all men, for that all have sinned."

Revelation 20:14–15: "And death and hell were cast into the lake of fire. This is the second death. And whosoever was not found written in the book of life was cast into the lake of fire."

Romans 5:17–19: "For if by one man's offence death reigned by one; much more they which receive abundance of grace and of the gift of righteousness shall reign in life by one, Jesus Christ. Therefore as by the offence of one judgment came upon all men to condemnation even so by the righteousness of one the free gift came upon all men unto justification of life. For as by one man's disobedience many were made sinners, so by the obedience of one shall many be made righteous."

Genesis 2:7, 22, and 1:27: "And the Lord God formed man of the dust of the ground, and breathed into his nostrils the breath of life; and man became a living soul. . . . And the rib, which the Lord God had taken from man, made he a woman, and brought her unto the man. . . . So God created man in his own image, in the image of God created he him; male and female created he them."

John 3:16–17: "For God so loved the world, that he gave his only begotten Son, that whosoever believeth in him should not perish, but have everlasting life. For God sent not his Son into the world to condemn the world; but that the world through him might be saved."

Luke 1:34–35: "Then said Mary unto the angel, 'How shall this be, seeing I know not a man?' And the angel answered and said unto her, 'The Holy Ghost shall come upon thee, and the power of the Highest shall overshadow thee; therefore also that holy thing which shall be born of thee shall be called the Son of God.'"

Matthew 1:20-25: "But while he thought on these things, behold, the angel of the Lord appeared unto him in a dream, saying, 'Joseph, thou son of David, fear not to take unto thee Mary thy wife; for that which is conceived in her is of the Holy Ghost. And she shall bring forth a son, and thou shalt call his name Jesus; for he shall save his people from their sins.' Now all this was done, that it might be fulfilled which was spoken of the Lord by the prophet, saying, 'Behold a virgin shall be with child, and shall bring forth a son, and they shall call his name Emanuel, which being interpreted is, God with us.' Then Joseph, being raised from sleep, did as the angel of the Lord had bidden him, and took unto him his wife: And knew her not till she had brought forth her firstborn son; and he called his name Jesus."

Hebrews 12:2: "Looking unto Jesus, the author and finisher of our faith; who for the joy that was set before him endured the cross, despising the shame, and is set down at the right hand of the throne of God."

Dear God,

Why did Eve let Satan trick her? Didn't she realize his presence when he shifted into the form of a snake dragon and started talking to her? I guess she didn't know that animals can't talk like humans when she met the serpent and didn't realize who it really was? Why did Lucifer want to do things disconnected from you anyway? You are right. I am feeling the same pull away from you but with me it is leading into a religious wonderland, making it hard for me to separate fantasy from reality. Help me please.

Genesis 3:1-7: "Now the serpent was more subtle than any beast of the field which the Lord God had made. And he said unto the woman, 'Yea, hath God said, "Ye shall not eat of every tree of the garden?"' And the woman said unto the serpent, 'We may eat of the fruit of the trees of the garden; but of the fruit of the tree which is in the midst of the garden, God hath said, "Ye shall not eat of it, neither shall ye touch it, lest ye die."' And the serpent said unto the worman, 'Ye shall not surely die; for God doth know that in the day ye eat thereof, then your eyes shall be opened, and ye shall be as gods, knowing good and evil.' And when the woman saw that the tree was good for food, and that it was pleasant to the eyes, and a tree to be desired to make one wise, she took of the fruit thereof, and did eat, and gave also unto her husband with her; and he did eat. And the eyes of them both were opened, and they knew that they were naked; and they sewed fig leaves together, and made themselves aprons."

Isaiah 14:12-15: "How art thou fallen from heaven, O Lucifer, son of the morning! How art thou cut down to the ground, which didst weaken the nations! For thou hast said in thine heart, 'I will ascend into heaven, I will exalt my throne above the stars of God; I will sit also upon the mount of the congregation, in the sides of the north; I will ascend above the heights of the clouds; I will be like the most High.' Yet thou shalt be brought down to hell, to the sides of the pit."

Dear God,
I don't see how Satan can possibly think he will defeat you, but I guess he thinks the time he has to fight you as your evil nemesis somehow makes him a type of god. I guess he thinks that anyone that chooses any form of evil over choosing a relationship with you becomes their own god instead of having you as their God. Satan seems to be taking advantage of the fact that you follow your own laws that keep you good and that you are who you are. Satan must know that if he could kill you everyone and everything would disappear and cease to exist because all things are sustained by you, but since he knows a time of judgment and punishment is coming for angels and humans who chose their way over yours, maybe he thinks killing you would be worth extinguishing everyone and everything.

I know it is a great privilege to be on your side in the fight between good and evil. I will be glad to be away from the fight with evil when I am in heaven with you, but while I am here, it is electrifying when you use me in one of your strategies, which always reflect your love, wisdom, power, and magnificence. You are always so tricky, but in a good way. You can always outthink anyone. You have *so* got this. I guess being on your side makes everything more than fair for your human children, because you are you, the one and only true God.

On the other hand, being in a world where evil always finds a way is very frightening and often keeps me on edge until I let you lead me into ways to refresh my spirit and soul. I try to always trust you, but it is often very scary down here. I'm not sure what is going on most of the time.

Second Timothy 1:7: "For God hath not given us the spirit of fear but of power, and of love, and of a sound mind."

Second Corinthians 10:5: "Casting down imaginations, and every high thing that exalteth itself against the knowledge of God, and bringing into captivity every thought to the obedience of Christ."

Dear God,
We share a love of books. I love to read. I love to read your Bible because I know you are trying to use it to transfer your thoughts to me, but now that I am in my sixties, I just thought I would have understood everything about living with you more by now. I love books because when I read them I feel I come to know the character of the people in the books. I get knowledge of their perspective. I get insights into my own thoughts,

feelings, and motivations by experiencing a part of life with them as they share their story in the place, time and perspective they are in. You are very honest about the stories of the people in the Bible that are trying to walk with you.

Dear Christie,
I love you. What is your point?

Dear God,
Don't you know? You must know. You know everything. I love you too.

Dear Christie,
Process please. Proceed please.
Second Timothy 3:16: "All Scripture is given by inspiration of God, and is profitable for doctrine, for reproof, for correction, for instruction in righteousness."

Dear God,
Finding you by reading my Bible is often challenging, but one summer day it presented an unexpected challenge for me. One fun thing about being a teacher is that we get off summers like the children do, and I get a lot of free time to swim in my above-ground pool and read. I was lying on my bed, happily reading the Bible, when a bug flew into my ear. It may have been a moth, I'm not sure. There was loud buzzing and crackling inside my head and I totally freaked out. I screamed for my son Ricky to help me. He was a teenager at the time. He poured alcohol in my ear over the sink to kill the bug and float it out. This seemed to work. I really appreciated his help, but I took great offense to his laughing the entire time he was helping me.

I went to the doctor the next day because I kept imagining pieces of the bug still in my ear. The doctor that walked in looked like she was about sixteen. Either she was a child genius or she really practices good health or she has great genes, or I am getting older. Maybe it is a combination of some of these, except for the getting older part, because if I am only as old as I feel in my heart, I am somewhere unrecorded as of yet since I spend a good portion of my days in La La Land along with my third-grade students.

Dear Christie,
Process Christie, please focus. Maybe you should make some other friends besides the children in your classroom.

Dear God,

Okay, I know only you live out of time and space and I have to joke about the funny things that happen to me as my body ages. I can laugh because I know someday you will give me an awesome, eternal, superwoman body in heaven. I know you will let me fly, right? I will be able to breathe underwater and walk through walls, right? I'm thinking I will never have to cook or clean or go to the bathroom. I will still be able to eat and never get fat, right? Jesus will dance with me over a rainbow, right?

Dear Christie,
Christie!
First Corinthians 6:13: "Meats for the belly, and the belly for meats; but God shall destroy both it and them. Now the body is not for fornication, but for the Lord; and the Lord for the body."
Revelation 19:9: "And he saith unto me, 'Write, "Blessed are they which are called unto the marriage supper of the Lamb."' And he saith unto me, 'These are the true sayings of God.'"

Dear God,
Yes, I am getting there. I know I am not wasting your time because you can listen to and develop me while listening to and developing everyone else that wants this at the same time. You are that awesome and amazing. You said our prayers were like sweet perfume to you. Right?
Psalm 141:2: "Let my prayer be set forth before thee as incense; and the lifting up of my hands as the evening sacrifice."

Dear Christie,
I never said that people never annoy me or make me angry. I just said that I always react with love and justice. I always do the right thing in each situation. I am patient. I love you. Get to your point.

Dear God,
Anyway the doctor looked in my ear with her thingy and said there was definitely not a bug in my ear and I saw her smile, though at least she was polite enough to try to hide it. She said since that didn't take long, she might as well give me my annual free physical, since I had accidentally skipped it for the last three years. She said I was at the age where I should have a blood test, mammogram, pap smear, and colonoscopy. I was wondering as she talked what the difference was between having all those tests done and being abducted and probed by aliens. Okay, I know aliens are not real.
Then she said, "Be honest, are you going to get a colonoscopy?"

I said, "No."

"Okay then," she said. "Take this envelope and put some feces in it and take it to a diagnostic clinic to have it analyzed."

I took the envelope and didn't tell her that I was not going to get any of these tests, unless I noticed a problem in any of these areas. I thought about the people receiving all these envelopes. I enjoy being a teacher, but sometimes it gets hard when there are conflicts, but at least I don't have to tell myself only 985 more poop specimens to look at before I get to go home. Thank you for the career you gave me.

Then she said that in the past all my numbers had looked good, except my weight numbers. What can I say, I'm a huggable grandma. She said I should be exercising every day. She asked me if I got any exercise last week. I told her that I had walked around a really big store. She typed something on her computer. So I guess that wasn't my best summer day. She did convince me to up my game a little with better eating habits and exercise though. Okay, I'll stop making excuses and listen to your guidance for better health habits. God, will you please help me with this as well?

Second Corinthians 4:16: "For which cause we faint not; but though our outward man perish, yet the inward man is renewed day by day."

Psalm 71:17-18: "O God, thou hast taught me from my youth; and hitherto have I declared thy wondrous works. Now also when I am old and grey-headed, O God, forsake me not; until I have shewed thy strength unto this generation, and thy power to every one that is to come."

Dear God,

I know we will all still be ourselves in heaven and yet not the same. We all have a lot more abilities, right? It will be nice to lose all the negative drama on this earth as we will all be centered in your love perspective without sin. I think all of our relationships with you, others, and ourselves will all be great, and the party will never end because the party is wherever you are.

Dear Christie,

Are you getting off point? Just stay close to me and you will be in a secure place with me no matter what your circumstances are.

Dear God,

I go in and out of that garden place with you.

Dear Christie,

Heaven is better than any of your dreams about it can be, mainly because you will never feel apart from me again, and your complete surrender to me that you will only have in heaven is the only way for you to really freely be you in my love and have complete happiness in our relationship and in your relationship with all others, yourself, and in life that is beyond your comprehension on this earth.

First Corinthians 2:9: "But as it is written, 'Eye hath not seen, nor ear heard, neither have entered into the heart of man, the things that God hath prepared for them that love him.'"

Dear Christie,

Now continue trying to figure this all out, but don't do it by getting off into circular worry loops and forgetting to trust me, because you may understand more and more and bit by bit, but you will never completely understand. You will begin to see things a lot more clearly in heaven, but as long as I let you remain on this earth, I have a purpose for you. I had a reason to allow earth time and to set it up the way I did, and this is such a short time compared to eternity, but this time will clearly show the destructiveness of evil and give any human who wants to become mine a chance to do so until the last human that I know is going to become mine does become mine, and then it will be finished. I have the patience to help you grow in wisdom, because I am God. I work as you are ready. I work slowly, patiently, and thoroughly with my children. I have eternity. I am eternal.

Dear God,

When you rebuke me, I know you only do it out of patience and love and for my good. I will get back on track. Let me summarize.

Dear Christie,

Why are you constantly repeating and summarizing?

Dear God,

I'm not sure, maybe it is because I have taught primary-age elementary school for so long. One day I just popped into this world completely clueless and sometimes now I feel almost as clueless. Is this really a game like hide-and-seek? Or is it more of a game like football? Is this a place of never-ending school, with never-ending tests that I have to take over and over if I fail until I finally pass and then I can move onto the next test? Is this a war? Exactly what did you pop me into? I wasn't here when you formed the world and I can't see beyond death. You used the genetic codes of my mom and dad to create me, and one day I was just here. I'm in the twenty-first century AD. Only you know the time you created the world and the time you will have for it's ending when evil will be gone and there will be a new eternal heaven and earth. The more I learn about you, the more there is to learn. You are unfathomable. You always have had a plan. You have thought everything through. I would say "from beginning to end," but with you there is no beginning or end, though there is a beginning and end to this earth and evil. Someday evil will simply be something we learned through experience and it will have no destructive consequences, pull, or power over us whatsoever. Thank you for this redemption.

Psalm 139:13–18: "For thou hast possessed my reins: thou hast covered me in my mother's womb. I will praise thee; for I am fearfully and wonderfully made; marvelous are thy works; and that my soul knoweth right well. My substance was not hid from thee, when I was made in secret, and curiously wrought in the lowest parts of the earth. Thine eyes did see my substance, yet being unperfect; and in thy book all my members were written, which in continuance were fashioned, when as yet there was none of them. How precious also are thy thoughts unto me, O God. How great is the sum of them. If I should count them, they are more in number than the sand; when I awake I am still with thee."

1 John 4:8: "He that loveth not, knoweth not God; for God is love."

Genesis 1:1: "In the beginning God created the heaven and the earth."

Genesis 2:2: "And on the seventh day God ended his work which he had made; and he rested on the seventh day from all his work which he had made."

Genesis 3:5: "For God doth know that in the day ye eat thereof, then your eyes shall be opened, and ye shall be as gods, knowing good and evil."

Genesis 3:15: "And I will put enmity between thee and the woman, and between thy seed and her seed; it shall bruise thy head, and thou shalt bruise his heel."

First Peter 3:7–10: "But the heavens and the earth, which are now, by the same word are kept in store, reserved unto fire against the day of judgment and perdition of ungodly men. But beloved, be not ignorant of this one thing, that one day is with the Lord as a thousand years, and a thousand years as one day. The Lord is not slack concerning his promise, as some men count slackness; but is longsuffering to usward, not willing that any should perish, but that all should come to repentance. But the day of the Lord will come as a thief in the night; in the which the heavens shall pass away with a great noise, and the elements shall melt with fervent heat, the earth also and the works that therein shall be burned up."

Isaiah 55:6–9: "Seek ye the Lord while he may be found, call ye upon him while he is near; let the wicked forsake his way, and the unrighteous man his thoughts; and let him return unto the Lord, and he will have mercy upon him; and to our God, for he will abundantly pardon. For my thoughts are not your thoughts, neither are your ways my ways, saith the Lord."

Romans 3:28: "Therefore we conclude that a man is justified by faith without the deeds of the law."

Dear Christie,
Is there anything else that you want to talk about that is confusing you right now?

Dear God,
Your laws also seem confusing at times. I guess I think you gave and give laws to us as protective boundaries against falling into the traps of the hurtfulness of evil so that we can have a better life on earth. I think you also give laws to us to show us that we are sinful and that we can never be good enough to make that connection to you ourselves. I think you want us to obey your laws to show the love link that you put in our heart with you when we came to you in repentance and faith. Rejecting your Holy Spirit's call to link with you is the only sin that will send a human to hell, but a lot of people start thinking linking to you is something they can do by obeying your laws, and then they think they can unlink themselves by disobeying your laws, and this keeps them from intimacy with you, even if they become your children.

Matthew 12:31-32: "And I tell you, every sin and blasphemy will be forgiven men, but the blasphemy against the Spirit will not be forgiven. Anyone who speaks a word against the Son of Man will be forgiven, but anyone who speaks against the Holy Spirit will not be forgiven, either in this age or in the age to come."

Matthew 6:33: "But seek ye first the kingdom of God, and his righteousness; and all these things shall be added unto you."

John 3:6-8: "That which is born of the flesh is flesh; and that which is born of the Spirit is spirit. Marvel not that I said unto thee, 'Ye must be born again.' The wind bloweth where it listeth, and thou hearest the sound thereof, but canst not tell whence it cometh, and whither it goeth; so is every one that is born of the Spirit."

First Timothy 2:4: "Who will have all men to be saved, and to come unto the knowledge of the truth."

Romans 1:17-20: "For therein is the righteousness of God revealed from faith to faith; as it is written, 'The just shall live by faith.' For the wrath of God is revealed from heaven against all ungodliness and unrighteousness of men, who hold the truth in unrighteousness; because that which may be known of God is manifest in them; for God hath shewed it unto them. For the invisible things of him from the creation of the world are clearly seen, being understood by the things that are made, even his eternal power and Godhead; so that they are without excuse."

John 3:3–5: "Jesus answered and said unto him, 'Verily, verily, I say unto thee, "Except a man be born again, he cannot see the kingdom of God."' Jesus answered, 'Verily, verily, I say unto thee, "Except a man be born of water and of the Spirit, he cannot enter into the kingdom of God."'"

Ephesians 2:8–9: "For by grace are ye saved through faith and that not of yourselves; it is the gift of God; not of works, lest any man should boast."

First Corinthians 5:8: "We are confident, I say, and willing rather to be absent from the body, and to be present with the Lord."

John 14:16–17: "And I will pray the Father, and he shall give you another Comforter that he may abide with you for ever; even the Spirit of truth; whom the world cannot receive, because it seeth him not, neither knoweth him; but ye know him; for he dwelleth with you, and shall be in you."

John 1:9: "That was the true Light, which lighteth every man that cometh into the world.

Genesis 3:15: "And I will put enmity between thee and the woman, and between thy seed and her seed; it shall bruise thy head, and thou shalt bruise his heel."

Dear God,

I can fellowship with any true believer in you who believes your Bible is all true and came to you in repentance and faith to become your child. We can just agree to disagree about everything else since you have such an individual plan for all of us.

Genesis 1:27: "So God created man in his own image, in the image of God created he him; male and female created he them."

Matthew 28:19: "Go ye therefore, and teach all nations, baptizing them in the name of the Father, and of the Son, and of the Holy Ghost."

Dear God,

I guess you put each person in the world, in the human family and in the time and place you put them in, because that is where they would have the best chance of individually deciding to connect with you, if they were ever going to make this decision. Your loving heart longs for each human to join your kingdom family, but you let each human decide for themselves.

Acts 17:24–29: "God that made the world and all things therein, seeing that he is Lord of heaven and earth, dwelleth not in temples made with hands; neither is worshipped with men's hands, as though he needed anything, seeing he giveth to all life, and breath, and all things; and hath made of one blood all nations of men for to dwell on all the face of the earth, and hath determined the times before appointed, and the bounds of their habitation; that they should seek the Lord, if haply they might feel after him, and find him, though he be not far from every one of us. For in him we live, and move, and have our being; as certain also of your own poets have said, for we are also his offspring. Forasmuch then as we are the offspring of God, we ought not to think that the Godhead is like unto gold, or silver, or stone, graven by art and man's device.

Dear God,

I was born before the internet. The internet and personal computers really got going when my son Ryan was a teen. He understood what it was all about right away and he loved it. He was explaining it to me and telling me his feelings about it. He said that there was information and communication flowing all around us, but that we had to have receptors in our computers to pick it up. He said that he wished that he had a receptor in his head so that the internet could just flow into his brain for him to pick up whatever he wanted.

I guess your information and communication is flowing all around us. When you make our spirit come alive and link to you, you give us a receiver in our spirit. Our spirit is connected to our soul and body. We hear your communication to us and we can communicate with you. You individualize and personalize your communication to each of us through your Holy Spirit. Your Holy Spirit interprets your data to us and listens to our prayers. We unblock ourselves for greater communication to and from you by confessing our sins to you and obeying you.

Your voice sounds like our own thoughts in our head and we have to decipher what thoughts are coming from you, and this is not always easy. I've figured out that your thoughts will never go against what your Bible says. Your thoughts may be hard, mind-blowing, exciting, or fun, but they will always be for our good and done with your loving best interest for us. Unfortunately, evil spirits also have the ability to enter into our minds, if we open a door for them to do so. Also, we have our own thoughts. Even though other people can't enter into our minds, their ideas that we read and hear from them can greatly influence us, and we have to be careful that we are always choosing your direction above anyone else's. Artists can powerfully influence us in ways that are not easy to understand. Ideas flow in stories, speeches, songs, pictures, and other art forms right into our hearts. I want to keep my heart true to you first. I never want to doubt the truth about your essence. I want to always know that surrendering my will to yours is the best way to go. Jesus, this is not easy.

Second Corinthians 10:5: "Casting down imaginations, and every high thing that exalteth itself against the knowledge of God, and bringing into captivity every thought to the obedience of Christ."

Following you makes me more free than robotic. A lot of people start thinking that if they really surrender to you that you will make them do something they hate with their life, like go and live in a hut in Africa as a missionary. The truth is that you call the people to be a missionary in Africa and to live in a hut because you know that they are the people that will love and light up with this kind of work. You call us to things that develop how you made us and light us up inside, even though we may not realize this is what we actually love doing until we surrender and do it your way. How you work things out is beyond my comprehension. You amaze me. Sometimes I think I may drive myself crazy trying to follow you, and then I find out that when I don't follow you, that becomes the time that I really go crazy inside. When I do follow you, I find peace and joy in your love, even when the world is going crazy around me. Who are you really? Who are you to me? Who are we together? Where are you?

Psalm 34:8: "O taste and see that the Lord is good; blessed is the man that trusteth in him."

Matthew 22:37–39: "Jesus said unto him, 'Thou shalt love the Lord thy God with all thy heart, and with all thy soul, and with all thy mind. This is the first and great commandment. And the second is like unto it, Thou shalt love thy neighbor as thyself.'"

Dear God,

A lot of people may think that these prayers are like me talking to an invisible six-foot pink bunny and having him talk back to me. They think you are an imaginary friend. They probably think the title of this book should be *My Imaginary God Bunny Friend*. What is even worse is if I start wondering if they are right. Sometimes I think evil spirits try to mess with my connection to you by telling me you are my imaginary friend and that you are like a giant, six-foot, pink, invisible bunny, especially people that say that there is no God and that the earth started from nothing and evolved over billions of years without you. Then I look around and see creation and I never see anything popping up from nothing or fossils that show one creature turning into another creature. I see the way you made life to adapt, appear self-sustaining and self-healing, but you made each species after its kind, and one species never turns into another species, even though that species may adapt and change as a species. You made all the animals in the garden, and the fossils show that the same species of animal are living today unless they became extinct. Out of all the planets and stars, how was this earth situated in just the right way to sustain life? I don't see how people can study science and believe in you less. The more I study science, the more I believe in you. It is just so illogical to not believe that someone beyond spectacular created and sustains all this. I guess another place you are hiding is in your creation. Also, when I stop letting your thoughts flow into my head, my inward joy turns very quickly into despair.

You came into my life and became my Father when I was about four years old, and though you have been invisible, you have never been imaginary. I will never come to the end of learning about you and growing in the love relationship that you have with me. What I do know about you keeps me trusting you as I progress through what I don't understand. If a person believes your Bible is true and has come to you in repentance and faith, I don't even argue about anything else we may agree or disagree on anymore, I'm just glad that there are other believers in the world trying to live their lives on your side the best they can.

Colossians 1:16–17: "For by him were all things created, that are in heaven, and that are in earth, visible and invisible, whether they be thrones, or dominions, or principalities, or powers; all things were created by him, and for him; And he is before all things, and by him all things consist."

Romans 8:14: "For as many as are led by the Spirit of God, they are the sons of God."

Dear Christie,

I want to communicate with you because I love you and your loving friendship is something I cannot have without you. I made angels and humans because I want to love and be loved. This whole thing is about having a love relationship with me. I set the world up for you to find me and connect with me and grow to understand more who I am. A relationship with me is like no other relationship. Part of choosing me means choosing my good will over evil.

Dear God,
Where are you?

Dear Christie,

I am in your heart, which is your life essence, your conscience, your Spirit and soul. I flow through your mind, will, emotions, and into your thoughts. Every sensation you feel, every move you make, and everything you do, I am there. No one was made to be more intimate with you than me. Don't you hear me? I gave you a spirit so that when it came alive and linked to me then you would have ears to hear me.

> Dear God,
> I want you to be real, but sometimes I have doubts and I become afraid that you, the one that fills my soul with love and joy, may not be real. Sometimes you seem too wonderful to be real. You are so awesome and I am not, but I guess you transform all your children to be able to hang with you in friendship, even though no one would be worthy without you. I think of why such a wonderful being would want to be in an intimate and transforming friendship with me. I don't want a God that I can imagine, dream up, or create. I don't want to live in my world as a schizophrenic, trying to block the imaginary to be able to live in reality and often not sure which is which and what is what. I want intimacy with the real you, no matter how fantastical I find you to truly be, and no matter how strange the path of faith often seems in this material, self-centered world, cursed by evil. You created me to only be happy when I am keeping you first in my life and my center, the same way you created all your angels and human beings when you gave them a spirit. I want this relationship with you, but sometimes I forget how to find you, even though you have me. You never disown me, but when I obey you I am closer to you, and when I disobey you I am further from you until I say I am sorry and surrender to you again. Why do you even want me? You are so much more than me.

> Dear Christie,
> I want you because you are mine. You want me because I am yours. Don't let the spirit enemy, who is always trying to take my place or keep any spirit beings from having a growing friendship with me, lie to you about who I am or about who you are connected to me. Don't get your identity from anyone or anything except me. You are awesome to me. You are a precious treasure to me.

> Dear God,
> After our morning conversation I drive to the beach with my son Ricky to meet my other son and his family. I put our conversation aside as I greet my family. I am at the beach in Florida, where I live. The ocean spray washes my face and I embrace and kiss my little grandchildren on their salty cheeks. My little grandchildren, Tony and Tina, are laughing and playing with my son Ryan, who is their dad, and their mom, Jillian, and their Uncle Ricky and me in the waves. Jillian just found out that she is pregnant again. The

puffy white clouds float in a sky of blue over our heads, where I imagine you are looking at us from behind those clouds or in those clouds and smiling with us. We can't see you. Can you see us? Did you give us family love partly to draw us toward your completing love?

The sunlight dances on the water, making the water look like it is full of sparkling diamonds. Seagulls dive into the waves, searching for fish. I hear their screech. I smell the fresh sea air blowing into my face. It doesn't make sense that all of this should have popped from nothing. Someone beyond amazing must have designed it and brought it into existence, I believe that someone was and is you. I'm so glad that I can teach at a school that wants to include you and tell the truth about you during each minute of the day.

I walk away from my playing family down the beach. I take a side path into a wooded nature reserve and I start talking with you, my God. You love getting into whatever mess I have gotten myself into and completely changing everything for me with your wisdom, healing, and loving power, from the inside out. I get into unhappy places that I know have no way out for me, except if you come and make a way out for me. I often feel lost and alone in the woods in more ways than one, especially when I see darkness pulling on the dear children that I teach and that I know you want for your own. You are pulling them toward finding real love and truth in you and you are using me, and I am glad.

Even in all this beauty, I sense evil's frightening presence working in the world and crawling in my head. There are so many other places that you let us freely choose that are not evil. Why does evil keep pulling on us humans, even when we feel its destruction? Only you know how to extinguish evil without extinguishing us. Nothing is too hard for you.

Job 34:14–15: "If he set his heart upon man if he gather unto himself his spirit and his breath; all flesh shall perish together and man shall turn again unto dust."

Ephesians 6:12: "For we wrestle not against flesh and blood, but against principalities, against powers, against the rulers of the darkness of this world, against spiritual wickedness in high places."

First Corinthians 4:6–7: "For God, who commanded the light to shine out of darkness, hath shined in our hearts, to give the light of the knowledge of the glory of God in the face of Jesus Christ. But we have this treasure in earthen vessels, that the excellency of the power may be of God, and not of us."

Revelation 2:11: "He that hath an ear, let him hear what the Spirit saith unto the churches; he that overcometh shall not be hurt of the second death."

Isaiah 55:6–11: "Seek ye the Lord while he may be found, call ye upon him while he is near; Let the wicked forsake his way, and the unrighteous man his thoughts; and let him return unto the Lord, and he will have mercy upon him; and to our God, for he will abundantly pardon. For my thoughts are not your thoughts, neither are your ways my ways, saith the Lord. For as the heavens are higher than the earth, so are my ways higher than your ways, and my thoughts than your thoughts. For as the rain cometh down, and the snow from heaven, and returneth not thither, but watereth the earth, and maketh it bring forth and bud, that it may give seed to the sower, and bread to the eater; so shall my word be that goeth forth out of my mouth; it shall not return unto me void, but it shall accomplish that which I please, and it shall prosper in the thing whereto I sent it.

Dear Christie,
You are who you are and I won't tell you to stop overthinking things and be more like another human. I love all of my children the same and I never made them to be identical to each other. You have to know though, only I completely understand why to overcome evil I had to turn into a perfect human to pay for the sins of all humans by letting myself be killed as a sacrifice, so that any human could have the chance to never have to go to hell. If I hadn't created hell, the universe would have turned evil, even I would have turned evil, and then there would be no hope. I am beyond sad that any angels or people ever have to go to hell. I want everyone at home with me, but love is a choice, and not everyone will choose to let me bring them home. There are my laws for me that I need to keep about good and evil that only I understand. I know and knew what I had to do to overcome evil forever and still have real friends, and I did it and am doing it for the joy of having an eternal, loving relationship with you and all my angel and people children.
Hebrews 12:2: "Looking unto Jesus the author and finisher of our faith; who for the joy that was set before him endured the cross, despising the shame, and is set down at the right hand of the throne of God."

Dear Christie,
You often bring up hell. We will talk more about this later. Don't let my justice keep you from seeing my love.

Dear God,
A lot of times your Bible seems to talk in extreme opposites, but I guess to find the meaning I have to look at the extremes like the bottom of a triangle and see that the real meaning can only be found at the top of the triangle in your thoughts. People can get very mixed up about what is evil and what is good, especially when tricky evil spirits are allowed to get

involved. We can get derailed because your Bible and ways are so hard to figure out without submitting to your Spirit's guidance.

Matthew 10:39: "He that findeth his life shall lose it; and he that loseth his life for my sake shall find it."

First John 4:1–10: "Beloved, believe not every spirit, but try the spirits whether they are of God; because many false prophets are gone out into the world. Hereby know ye the Spirit of God; every spirit that confesseth that Jesus Christ is come in the flesh is of God; and every spirit that confesseth not that Jesus Christ is come in the flesh is not of God; and this is that spirit of antichrist, whereof ye have heard that it should come; and even now already is in the world. Ye are of God, little children, and have overcome them; because greater is he that is in you, than he that is in the world. They are of the world; therefore speak they of the world, and the world heareth them. We are of God; he that knoweth God heareth us; he that is not of God heareth not us. Hereby know we the spirit of truth, and the spirit of error. Beloved, let us love one another; for love is of God; and every one that loveth is born of God, and knoweth God. He that loveth not knoweth not God; for God is love. In this was manifested the love of God toward us, because that God sent his only begotten Son into the world, that we might live through him. Herein is love, not that we loved God, but that he loved us, and sent his Son to be the propitiation for our sins."

Romans 5:18–19: "Therefore, as by the offence of one judgment came upon all men to condemnation; even so by the righteousness of one the free gift came upon all men unto justification of life. For as by one man's disobedience many were made sinners, so by the obedience of one shall many be made righteous."

Second Peter 3:8: "But, beloved, be not ignorant of this one thing, that one day is with the Lord as a thousand years, and a thousand years as one day."

Dear Christie,

Please hear my voice talking in your spirit and let me come into your mess and heal our connection. You are looking for me. Find me.

Dear God,

As I look into the woods I am lost in, I see dancing demons in my imagination. They are playing flutes to the tune that each individual wants to hear to keep people from becoming your children or to keep your children from becoming close with you. The tune they are playing for me is a longing for comfort and ease before God brings me out of the battle and before God brings me home. People are following these demons, who appear as angels of light, over the cliff into hell. The illusions are all there right to the point of their death and then they are enveloped in the darkness of soul sleep until the judgment when they will serve their time of punishment in hell until they are burned completely away in hell, because they chose to replace you with anyone or anything. Someday their fallen angel friends will join them there to serve their punishment until they are also burned completely away. Immortality can only come to those linked to you.

Hebrews 12:27-29: "And this word, yet once more, signifieth the removing of those things that are shaken. As of things that are made, that those things which cannot be shaken may remain. Wherefore we receive a kingdom which cannot be moved, let us have grace, whereby we may serve God acceptably with reverence and godly fear; for our God is a consuming fire."

Matthew 22:30: "For in the resurrection they neither marry, nor are given in marriage, but are as the angels of God in heaven."

Luke 1:37: "For with God nothing shall be impossible."

First Corinthians 13:9-13: "For we know in part, and we prophesy in part. But when that which is perfect is come, then that which is in part shall be done away. When I was a child, I spake as a child, I understood as a child, I thought as a child; but when I became a man, I put away childish things. For now we see through a glass, darkly; but then face to face now I know in part; but then shall I know even as also I am known. And now abideth faith, hope, charity (love), these three; but the greatest of these is charity (love)."

Philippians 4:6-8: "Be careful for nothing; but in every thing by prayer and supplication with thanksgiving let your requests be made known unto God. And the peace of God, which passeth all understanding, shall keep your hearts and minds through Christ Jesus. Finally, brethren, whatsoever things are true, whatsoever things are honest, whatsoever things are just, whatsoever things are pure, whatsoever things are lovely, whatsoever things are of good report; if there be any virtue, and if there be any praise, think on these things."

Dear God,
Having my way now is not worth having it at the expense of losing intimacy with you. I thought I would have a lot more knowledge, friends, riches, fame, power, comfort, and a lot of other things by this age in my life. Whatever you want me to have or not to have during each stage of my life is fine as long as I have you. There are no regrets with you because you turn everything in each of your childrens' lives to flow into your perfect will. There is no friend like you. You are life. You are love.

I guess I wanted out of the battle of good versus evil before you actually choose in your time to take me out of the battle. I will be out of the battle when my body dies and my spirit and soul comes to you, but then I won't have an opportunity to be in the game anymore. I have to admit, being on your team often brings me my greatest moments of euphoria as I connect with you as you run your magnificent plays, even though sometimes they come after completely terrifying and disgusting moments of evil confrontations where I am gripping your hand very tightly. I sometimes feel the pull to give up the struggle and sink into the dark side inside myself. Instead you want me to remember that evil is the true enemy of us all and only your love and wisdom have the power to lead us out of the strangleholds it can put our lives in, keeping us from engaging in your love. Your perfect will will be accomplished in all your children, but we may miss out on getting to do some of the things you planned for us to do for the times another heart was willing and ours wasn't. The material world of money, power, fame, popularity, fulfillment apart from you, and anything outside of your kingdom will always hurt and fade if we pursue it instead of pursuing your guidance. I want you to be the dream I dream.

I want to give up wanting my will above your will because it causes me to lose my closeness with you. Living the life you want me to live is impossible, but surrendering my will to you as you step me through life right where I am at to where you have me going is possible. I surrender to your Spirit. I constantly give my evil to you, even knowing that I am not rid of it. You are not asking for the impossibility of my perfection, but just my constant surrender back to you in my back-and-forth imperfection. I can never make choices that keep me from accomplishing your perfect will in my life, because you have the power to always redirect my path as long as I am constantly confessing and surrendering and trying to follow your will, step-by-step, without knowing the way. You know the way. You see the big picture. You live in light of eternity. I need to keep your GPS turned on just like I keep it turned on when I am in my car and I don't have any idea where I am going. If I make several different turns, the GPS will guide me from where I am at to still be able to reach my destination. Your Holy Spirit is like my GPS, guiding me through my life's journey. You, the Trinity, will always get me to my final destination no matter how many confused turns I take. You will always instantly redirect me into your plans along my journey to my final destination as soon as I turn my GPS back on by confession and surrender.

The enemy is attacking the family unit you established to try to lead people away from your love. Sometimes as I teach little children, I seriously feel these effects with them. The Evil Spirit has many forms of attack. He will try to bring in as many dysfunctions as possible. All children have hardships, some more than others, but if they become yours and let you guide them, they have everything that they will ever need to travel through this world in the bubble of your love out of evil and into your home in the next world.

The three main places we Christians seem to have to guide children toward you is in the family, the church, and the Christian school. We so often lead children toward a relationship with religion instead of a relationship with you.

Proverbs 22:6: "Train up a child in the way he should go; and when he is old, he will not depart from it."

Malachi 2:15: "And did not he make one? Yet had he the residue of the spirit. And wherefore one? That he might seek a godly seed. Therefore, take heed to your Spirit, and let none deal treacherously against the wife of his youth."

First Corinthians 7:13–15: "And the woman which hath a husband that believeth not, and if he be pleased to dwell with her, let her not leave him. For the unbelieving husband is sanctified by the wife, and the unbelieving wife is sanctified by the husband; else were your children unclean; but now are they holy. But if the unbelieving depart, let him depart. A brother or a sister is not under bondage in such cases; but God hath called us to peace."

I thought maybe a Christian school would be like this perfect little factory where the children went in in kindergarten and rolled out in twelfth grade as perfect Christians and everyone involved with them just did their jobs always with wisdom, maturity, happiness, and love overflowing. Why do I have to have any physical, emotional, relational, spiritual, or self-identity hardships still? Why does anyone have problems that are involved in this ministry? It is probably the invisible spiritual battle going on, right?

Luke 6:35–38: "But love ye your enemies, and do good, and lend, hoping for nothing again; and your reward shall be great, and ye shall be the children of the Highest; for he is kind unto the unthankful and to the evil. Be ye therefore merciful, as your Father also is merciful. Judge not, and ye shall not be judged; condemn not, and ye shall not be condemned, forgive, and ye shall be forgiven. Give, and it shall be given unto you; good measure, pressed down, and shaken together, and running over, shall men give into your bosom. For with the same measure that ye meet withal it shall be measured to you again."

Matthew 24:12: "And because iniquity shall abound, the love of many shall wax cold."

I was always drawn toward being a teacher, even as a child. When I was in college, you gave me a vision. I had a vision of Jesus standing at the front of a large crowd asking who would go into Christian schools to teach for him. I was jumping up and down and shouting, "Pick me!"

I was at the back of the large crowd and I never thought Jesus would see me or pick me. Then Jesus grew taller and larger and leaned over the crowd and pointed at me and said, "Okay, I pick you."

I was completely thrilled. I have been so glad to teach children about you in every subject in Christian schools for almost forty years now. I have always loved interacting with children, and I still do. They are humorous and joyful to me. Children seem to always put love connection as their first priority and always having fun as their second priority. They haven't yet been programmed to think in the group mentality way and they are very creative. They have trusting and open hearts. They are willing to try and learn new things. I see why you said that we need this type of mindset to decide to enter your kingdom. I love working with children most of the time, and I call on you for those hard times.

Luke 18:16–17: "But Jesus called them unto him, and said, 'Suffer little children to come unto me, and forbid them not; for of such is the kingdom of God. Verily I say unto you, "Whosoever shall not receive the kingdom of God as a little child shall in no wise enter therein."'"

You have also used this ministry you put me in to allow me to send my sons to Christian schools and provide needed finances. I still need money for Ricky for college. My husband is disabled and on social security disability and I don't see any way that I can stop working and retire right now. You've given me the health and strength to work in the classroom and at home and most of the time I really enjoy all of it, except maybe doing the dishes. You've always helped me to pay my bills and get to a nice middle-class life. I need to start thanking you for your blessings and look at the good you bring to my life instead of always letting my mind rove into complaining and discontentment. You never promise that being your child means that we will be or won't be rich monitarily, but you do promise to always provide for the needs of each of your children until it is time for them to die. You choose to allow trials and blessings in each individual life of people, whether they are your children or not, because you have your reasons that I don't think we will ever really understand while we live on this earth. However, we believers have you to guide us through and you work secret blessing-miracles for us as we pray, and you grow a friendship with us, and you transform us inside, and you take us to heaven when we die. I wish everyone had you, and I know you do, too. You may communicate with us in a verse or a song or a vision or a dream or a sermon or a persistent thought in our minds or an insight we gain that we just know is from you as we travel along on our earthly journey, with all its ups and downs and twists and turns. You can use anyone or anything to give us messages but we learn to identify your voice with faith from our spirit connection to your Spirit. I guess you are hiding in the messages that you bring to each of your children as you communicate to us in your completely unique way.

Dear God,

I am sorry that I have become angry that I am not retired right now with a huge amount of money and with no problems, except what to do for fun each day. You know me better than I know myself, and your will is what truly lights me up. I changed my mind. I don't want heaven on earth. I am happy that you will let me live with you in heaven after I die, and I just want to be close to you while I am on this earth through any good or bad times I need to travel through. I would probably be totally miserable if I got my way now anyway by sitting in a beach mansion with excellent health, a lot of money, surrounded by family and friends, and with servants to do everything hard for me. Sorry. You are better than material things. You make me happier than anyone or anything. Only you know what truly makes me happy, and you, plus doing what you want, are my greatest desire. Actually, nothing lights me up more inside than sitting in a room, interacting with little children all day, and teaching them about you and your wonders. My mom thinks I'm crazy. You made us all so different.

I am glad you are supplying me with the health and wisdom to continue to do this in this ever-changing technological world, and using my job to help meet the money needs of my family for now. You always supply my needs and you only supply my wants that you choose to supply with me, for the reasons you choose, and they are always great. Thanks for always getting me back on track to get close to you again, because being close to you is worth everything, like all the people who gave their lives because they weren't willing to give up closeness to you realized. I am grateful, though, that I do not live in a time and a place where they throw Christians to lions. This earth is nothing compared to heaven, and it is a much shorter time than eternity, so I would rather have heaven later without evil than now while I am fighting evil with you, if I had to make a choice. Keep bringing the people, strength, and wisdom into my life to help me keep doing your will, which is always what is best for me. Help me have more trust and contentment in you. Help me to be more grateful for all your blessings and not be angry at you for the evil that is in the world. Thank you for my life. I love you.

Philippians 4:19: "But my God shall supply all your needs according to his riches in glory by Christ Jesus."

Zechariah 4:6: "Then he answered and spake unto me, saying, 'This is the word of the Lord unto Zerubbabel, saying, "Not by might, nor by power, but by my spirit," saith the Lord of hosts.'"

Job 5:2: "For wrath killeth the foolish man, and envy slayeth the silly one."

God, when I am real with you, why are you always changing my attitude instead of my circumstances? I guess it is true what I tell the children in my class, which is, "Stinky attitude, stinky life. Good attitude, good life." Help me be content with how you made me and how you lead me. Let me get my identity from you and be happy in it.

Romans 9:20: "Nay, but, O man, who art thou that repliest against God? Shall the thing formed say to him that formed it, 'Why hast thou made me thus?'"

Every time I start complaining to you in prayer, you somehow change my point of view to yours. It seems very tricky, but I'm very glad you do it. Your joy again floods into my soul, and my dark thoughts become happy. I start to feel less lost, inside and outside, as I hold your hand to guide me.

I look out and find my way out of the woods because I see the ocean glimmering through the trees. I only have to get back to the beach and then I can find my family again. As I walk back along the edge of the ocean, I see the ocean horizon that is touching the sky and think of all your wonders that I see on my beach walk. I see smiling dolphins leaping and playing as they swim together. I see shark fins. I see birds diving in the water to get fish. I see schools of manatees swimming and redirecting themselves quickly when they meet any obstacle. I see sandpipers running along the water's edge. I hear the ocean roar and feel the splash of the waves on my feet. You are so creative and orderly and synchronized at the same time. You share. You are humorous. You did make crabs. You are playful. You did make children. You are so amazing.

It seems like family love is a high priority for humans and you use this to point humans toward you. You give us examples of yourself as being like a good and loving father and husband and all of us believers being blessed to be your children. That is probably one reason that Satan tries to get everyone and anyone to practice sex other than the way you wanted humans to practice it, which is one man and one woman for life. Satan knows that if humans give into this pull, it is one of the best ways to disrupt a family.

I think about the family you put me in as I head back to them from my walk on the beach. Some of them are here at the beach, and some are not. I guess most of my personal family's racial ancestors and my ancestors would be mostly of European descent. I guess truly, racially, we are mutts like most Americans. You placed me in Florida, in the United States of America, in the twenty-first century. You gave me myself with a body, soul, and spirit. You gave me a mother and father. They tried to help people find you by being a minister and a minister's wife. My father is now with you.

You gave me a sister, Serena, who has adopted eleven children from rough homes and tried to mother them toward you. She did this most of her life as a single person and she is amazing. My brother, Tommy, and his wife raised their three children to find love and joy in you. Their children are passing this along to their own families now.

You gave me a husband, Barry, for over forty years now. He has enabled my sons and I to develop and do what we individually think is most important in life. You gave us our grown son Ryan. He is married to our daughter-in-law, Jillian. Ryan and Jillian are beautiful lights for you in every way and they are passing your love along to my two young grandchildren, Tony and Tina. Please help Tony and Tina and the new baby who is coming to link their spirit with yours as soon as they are ready. You gave me a son that is about to enter college named Ricky. Ricky is a strong Christian and a very good friend to me. He is a joy to Barry and I in every way. Our sons seem so amazingly smart and accomplished to Barry and I, since we never really felt we knew exactly what we were doing as parents. We know that the reason they are the way they are is because they both surrendered to you early in life and keep surrendering to you through their lives. They are so beautiful because of you.

You gave me little third-grade children to teach in my classroom in the Christian school I teach in. Children light me up inside. I love teaching them and interacting with them. I'm glad you let me be a Christian elementary teacher in varying Christian schools for decades. I have mostly worked in the primary grades. I like these grades because they are such foundational years for you to draw believing hearts to you and your ways. In Christian schools, we are freely allowed to talk out loud about you and to you all day. I thank you for this. But more than anyone or anything else, I thank you for giving me yourself.

Hebrews 13:5: "Let your conversation be without covetousness; and be content with such things as ye have; for he hath said, 'I will never leave thee, nor forsake thee.'"

You are always with me whether my feelings perceive you or not, and I am happy to feel connected to you again. Even though I am always connected, I am happier when I feel it. I want your will more than my own because I want to be close to you and you know best.

I am back to my family after wandering on the beach, and my family and I begin flipping through the sticky sand to go to our car and drive home after another fun day from you. The interplay between shadows and light on the setting day is fun to watch on the surrounding nature and people.

The palm trees turn to shadows. You used a tree to allow us to bring evil in and you died on a tree to free us from evil's curse. You have a tree in heaven to symbolize the eternal life you will give us. You live out of time, but you created time for us. You are immaterial, but you place us in a material world to learn about you and to learn to hate evil like you do. You give us clues, prophets, a book, and your Spirit in our thoughts to learn how to begin and grow a relationship with you. You come into our very consciousness, heart, soul, spirit, whatever the term, to make us yours and develop your friendship with us, and I guess there is no better place than that. Every day in heaven will be better than the best day ever was here because everyone and everything will always be totally centered on you.

Even the elements of your world seem to reflect the relationship you want with us. You are like fire, God, the Holy Spirit is like the wind, Jesus is like water, and humans are like the soil that our bodies will turn back into when we die. Even the melanin you used to make the varying shades of the color brown that you used in each human's skin color reflects the varying shades of the earth's soil colors (red, yellow, tan, and black), reminding us that you made the first man, whom all humans have descended from, from the soil.

Ricky and I wave goodbye and head home in our car to Barry. You talk to me as I drive in the darkness as Ricky puts his handsome head back and takes a nap.

First Corinthians 13:9-13: "For we know in part, and we prophesy in part. But when that which is perfect is come, then that which is in part shall be done away. When I was a child, I spake as a child, I understood as a child, I thought as a child; but when I became a man, I put away childish things. For now we see through a glass, darkly; but then face to face; now I know in part; but then shall I know even as also I am known. And now abideth faith, hope, charity (love), these three; but the greatest of these is charity (love)."

Dear Christie,

You are welcome to keep trying to figure things out existentially and ontologically as long as you know that if I truly downloaded all my knowledge on you, you would explode. Also, I give different gifts and insights to each of my children so that they will have the unity of love, sort of like a body, with me as the head, in reflecting and carrying out my will in the way I created them to carry it out. Work it through the best you can as long as you keep having faith in me and in the truth of my Bible. I love you and I am glad you are back in the garden with me.

Dear God,

I am so happy to be close with you. I love you. Help me keep finding you in all of your hiding places.

Matthew 25:41, 46: "Then shall he say also unto them on the left hand, Depart from me, ye cursed, into everlasting fire, prepared for the devil and his angels . . . and these shall go away into everlasting punishment; but the righteous into life eternal."

Second Peter 2:12: "But these, as natural brute beasts, made to be taken and destroyed, speak evil of the things that they understand not; and shall utterly perish in their own corruption."

Matthew 10:28: "And fear not them which kill the body, but are not able to kill the soul; but rather fear him which is able to destroy both soul and body in hell."

Second Corinthians 5:6–7: "Therefore we are always confident, knowing that, whilst we are at home in the body, we are absent from the Lord; for we walk by faith, not by sight."

First Corinthians 15:50–54: "Now this I say, brethren, that flesh and blood cannot inherit the kingdom of God; neither doth corruption inherit incorruption. Behold, I shew you a mystery; we shall not all sleep, but we shall all be changed. In a moment, in the twinkling of an eye, at the last trump; for the trumpet shall sound, and the dead shall be raised incorruptible, and we shall be changed. For this corruptible must put on incorruption, and this mortal must put on immortality. So when this corruptible shall have put on incorruption, and this mortal shall have put on immortality, then shall be brought to pass the saying that is written, 'Death is swallowed up in victory.'"

Hebrews 12:27: "And this word, yet once more, signifieth the removing of those things that are shaken, as of things that are made, that those things which cannot be shaken may remain."

Psalm 66:4: "All the earth shall worship thee, and shall sing unto thee; they shall sing to thy name. *Selah.*"

Psalm 67:2: "That thy way may be known upon earth, thy saving health among all nations."

Hebrews 1:1–3: "God, who at sundry times and in divers manners spake in time past unto the fathers by the prophets, hath in these last days spoken unto us by his Son, whom he hath appointed heir of all things, by whom also he made the worlds; who being the brightness of his glory, and the express image of his person, and upholding all things by the word of his power, when he had by himself purged our sins, sat down on the right hand of the Majesty on high."

First Corinthians 2:5–14: "That your faith should not stand in the wisdom of men, but in the power of God. Howbeit we speak wisdom among them that are perfect; yet not the wisdom of this world, not of the princes of this world, that come to nought; but we speak the wisdom of God in a mystery, even the hidden wisdom, which God ordained before the world unto our glory; but as it is written, 'Eye hath not seen, nor ear heard, neither have entered into the heart of man, the things which God hath prepared for them that love him.' But God hath revealed them unto us by his Spirit; for the Spirit searcheth all things, yea, the deep things of God. For what man knoweth the things of a man, save the spirit of man which is in him? Even so the things of God knoweth no man, but the Spirit of God. Now we have received, not the spirit of the world, but the spirit which is of God; that we might know the things that are freely given to us of God. Which things also we speak, not in the words which man's wisdom teacheth, but which the Holy Ghost teacheth; comparing spiritual things with spiritual. But the natural man receiveth not the things of the Spirit of God; for they are foolishness unto him; neither can he know them, because they are spiritually discerned."

Galatians 2:16, 21: "Knowing that a man is not justified by the works of the law, but by the faith of Jesus Christ, even we have believed in Jesus Christ, that we might be justified by the faith of Christ, and not by the works of the law; for by the works of the law shall no flesh be justified. . . . I do not frustrate the grace of God; for if righteousness come by the law, then Christ is dead in vain."

First Peter 4:6: "For for this cause was the gospel preached also to them that are dead, that they might be judged according to men in the flesh, but live according to God in the spirit."

Romans 8:3: "For what the law could not do, in that it was weak through the flesh, God sending his own Son in the likeness of sinful flesh, and for sin, condemned sin in the flesh."

Psalm 16:11: "Thou wilt shew me the path of life; in thy presence is fullness of joy; at thy right hand there are pleasures for evermore."

Psalm 17:15: "As for me, I will behold thy face in righteousness; I shall be satisfied, when I awake, with thy likeness."

James 1:17: "Every good gift and every perfect gift is from above, and cometh down from the Father of lights, with whom is no variableness, neither shadow of turning."

Deuteronomy 30:19–20: "I call heaven and earth to record this day against you, that I have set before you life and death, blessing and cursing; therefore choose life, that both thou and thy seed may live; that thou mayest love the Lord thy God, and that thou mayest obey his voice, and that thou mayest cleave unto him; for he is thy life, and the length of thy days; that thou mayest dwell in the land which the Lord sware unto thy fathers, to Abraham, to Isaac, and to Jacob, to give them.

John 3:3–8, 16: "Jesus answered and said unto him, 'Verily, verily, I say unto thee, except a man be born again, he cannot see the kingdom of God.' Nicodemus saith unto him, 'How can a man be born when he is old? Can he enter the second time into his mother's womb, and be born?' Jesus answered, 'Verily, verily, I say unto thee, except a man be born of water and of the Spirit, he cannot enter into the kingdom of God. That which is born of the flesh is flesh; and that which is born of the Spirit is spirit. Marvel not that I said unto thee, "Ye must be born again." The wind bloweth where it listeth, and thou hearest the sound thereof, but canst not tell whence it cometh, and whither it goeth; so is every one that is born of the Spirit.' . . . 'For God so loved the world, that he gave his only begotten Son, that whosoever believeth in him should not perish, but have everlasting life.'"

Genesis 3:15: "And I will put enmity between thee and the woman, and between thy seed and her seed; it shall bruise thy head, and thou shalt bruise his heel."

Romans 5:17: "For if by one man's offence death reigned by one; much more they which receive abundance of grace and of the gift of righteousness shall reign in life by one, Jesus Christ."

Hebrews 11:4: "By faith Abel offered unto God a more excellent sacrifice than Cain by which he obtained witness that he was righteous, God testifying of his gifts; and by it he being dead yet speaketh."

Second Corinthians 5:17–21: "Therefore if any man be in Christ, he is a new creature; old things are passed away; behold, all things are become new. And all things are of God, who hath reconciled us to himself by Jesus Christ, and hath given to us the ministry of reconciliation; to wit, that God was in Christ, reconciling the world unto himself, not imputing their trespasses unto them; and hath committed unto us the word of reconciliation. Now then, we are ambassadors for Christ, as though God did beseech you by us; we pray you in Christ's stead, be ye reconciled to God. For he hath made him to be sin for us, who knew no sin; that we might be made the righteousness of God in him."

Romans 3:20-26: "Therefore by the deeds of the law there shall no flesh be justified in his sight; for by the law is the knowledge of sin. But now the righteousness of God without the law is manifested, being witnessed by the law and the prophets; Even the righteousness of God which is by faith of Jesus Christ unto all and upon all them that believe; for there is no difference; for all have sinned, and come short of the glory of God; being justified freely by his grace through the redemption that is in Christ Jesus, whom God hath set forth to be a propitiation through faith in his blood, to declare his righteousness for the remission of sins that are past, through the forbearance of God; to declare, I say, at this time, his righteousness; that he might be just, and the justifier of him which believeth in Jesus."

Dear Christie,
You are home now. Go to bed. I'll talk to you in the morning.

Goodnight God,
Ricky and I are going into the house now and cleaning up. Ricky and I are saying goodnight. Ricky is so young, strong, wise, and handsome. Please God, help Ricky to stay strongly connected to you all of his life that passes through in a blink of eternity.

Now I am snuggling down with Barry, the old man you gave me. He is snuggling down with the old woman you gave him: me. It is nice to have someone to snuggle with. Old age reflects to us that you did not make us immortal. This can be a pointer toward finding and connecting with your eternal love.

Barry and I remember when we were young. All the stages of life we lived through together flit in and out of our memories as we embrace. Every stage of human life has its good points and challenges. The blessings of extreme strength and beauty are given to humans in their young adult lives. These blessings are fleeting here but will be eternal when we are in heaven with you and have our immortal bodies. Sometimes this earth time almost seems like a shadow dream that is fading away into the reality of the world we will one day share with you. That world will never fade and will be free of all nightmares. I remember when Barry and I were dating and we were at the beach and his strong arms lifted me right out of the water over his head, and then he threw me in the water. Then we hugged and laughed and kissed underwater. When we stood up his black hair and mustache glistened in the sun. He was so young and strong and happy. I was also young and well-shaped and beautiful.

Barry is disabled now after his triple bypass. Thank you that he is stable now, even though his energy never came back and he walks with a walker. It is nice to still have someone to snuggle with. I'm glad he didn't die quite yet. We may not be what we used to be, but we love each other because we belong to each other, he is mine and I am his in a special way. That is what you were telling me about you and me today. We love each other because we belong to each other. I am yours and you are mine in a uniquely special way—that is what you meant marriage to reflect. However, there is no relationship that can take the place of the relationship between you and each of your human children because that is the only relationship that makes us real.

Thank you for always being there personally for me and for all of your children in heaven and on earth. You are so awesome that you can be a personal God for us all at the same time.

I guess you are hiding in my surrendered obedience to you. I obey and surrender because I know your character is love, just, and you always know best. I would rather do things your way than mine, even when I wouldn't rather, because I find the real you in that place and I find the real me in that place and we play and laugh and have adventures in that wonderful place of friendship in our secret garden. I love you, God.

If you want me to keep seeking you all the time in this earthly life, I will. Now that I have figured out a lot of your hiding places, it will make it a lot easier.

Jeremiah 29:13: "And ye shall seek me, and find me, when ye shall search for me with all your heart."

Goodnight Christie.
Maybe you are finally starting to get it in your sixties.

Dear God,
Thank you for not saying it is about time.

Dear Christie,
I love you.

Chapter Two

Angels versus Demons

    Yin and Yang, black and white, we are all born into this fight.
God is pulling people out of it all, he wants each human to answer his call.
The fallen spirit world encourages all god posers to break away from God to do their thing.
Only God and God's power rides higher than anyone or anything, including yin and yang, and only in him can real truth and life ring.

    Dear God,

Since you, the spirit world, and my own spirit are invisible to my five senses, I am trying to imagine the best I can what is really going on by trying to listen to your Spirit in my thoughts and when I read your Bible, and by listening to Christians talking about their life journey with you, and by observing life through reading and experience. Unfortunately, I've probably learned more than I wanted to learn about fallen angel demons by making friends with them. They are not good friends and they often sneak in my back door, even when I have shut and locked my front door. They know who I am and what I like and what I don't like. They know my strengths and weaknesses and my emotional makeup and the psychology of me. Please help me shut all the doors to them and only open the doors to your Holy Spirit to talk in my thoughts. Since they know people don't see the whole picture while they are on the earth, since you set the world up so people will only be able to find you with repentance and faith here, they try to use this to get unbelievers to never find you and believers to get lost in their own imagination.

All of us believers need to stick together in fellowship, so the evil spirits don't get us fighting each other instead of shining your light in the darkness for others to find you. When we are in heaven, the denominations each of us belonged to will fade into unimportance. As long as a believer believes your Bible is all true and that the only way to become your child is through repentance to you and faith in you, I'm not going to fight about all the different parts of the Bible that we are all trying to understand in the best way we can. We have to be content with knowing that we will never get the completely clear picture this side of heaven, and we need to trust you as we keep trying to find and follow your individual guidance, communication, and will for us for each minute of every day. We need to agree to let our disagreements go back to you. I used to argue about my opinions all the time and my pride and anger blocked others from seeing you. Now I see that you would much rather have me share love and care for others than to cram my subjective opinions down their throats. I need to encourage the good I see in others and just work out my thoughts and opinions with you, because all of us will have surprises in heaven as we really see how truly mind-blowing you are. We can all stimulate each other to go to you and your Bible to try to think about things and figure things out, but as long as we have the most important thing down by becoming your child, every other honest interpretation that we try to make about the Bible can be placed at your feet, since you are truth and you have eternity to help us learn more and more about you and your truth. We will never stop developing with you as the piece of your body that we are, because we will always be the person you designed us to be in our mother's womb, and we will never be you, because there is only one you, but you made us amazing enough to absorb truth coming from your perspective into our own perspective.

Second Corinthians 10:5: "Casting down imaginations, and every high thing that exalteth itself against the knowledge of God, and bringing into captivity every thought to the obedience of Christ;"

Dear God,
I will tell you how I imagine that demons and angels interact in the dimension that is invisible to us humans from using the true stories of people I have known in my dad's church. I'm not sure how much I am getting right or wrong, but here is my daydream of these beings of shadows and light.

I see my friends, Rob and Maria, in China. I am daydreaming about how things might have been for my friends from the United States when they lived in China twenty years ago as undercover missionaries. I met them when they attended my dad's church before they became missionaries. I sent them a small sum every month to help with their funding. I'm thinking back in time to how I pictured things were for them as I prayed for them.

Rob is a medical doctor, and the Chinese government let him into their country with his wife and three children so he could help develop medical programs for China. He is a Chinese American and his Chinese descent helped him get into this program where he hopes to shine a light toward God for his ancestral people. His wife is Hispanic and she is also American. She loves God and is willing to support her husband's call from God. Their three children speak both Chinese and English fluently. Their whole family has developed a deep love for the land of China and the Chinese people, and they want them to know God. This is my daydream about what went on in the spirit world while Rob and Maria were in China:

Rob and Maria are standing in a small room, talking with three Chinese women. Rob is giving them medical attention and advice while Maria is standing to the side, assisting when necessary.

Rob is thinking, "It was hard leaving the United States a few months ago after our last furlough. There is so much space in the United States, unlike the overcrowding here. Also, here I have a restricted income. I could have a huge house with a pool and woods around it instead of all the small, cramped apartments we have always had to live in in China. Everywhere you turn here is crowded with people. I could have a big luxurious car instead of the bicycles we have to ride here. We have never been able to use cars because almost everyone uses only bicycles. I worry about Maria and our children being hurt riding bikes in such crowded conditions. Instead of worrying about the funds coming in, I could have so much more money if I had stayed in the United States as a doctor. Also, my dad is not feeling well and could move into my home and I could take care of him if I still lived in the States. He has been lonely since my mom died. I need God to turn my thoughts back to the heart of love he placed in me to help these people spiritually and medically. I will pray for this."

Maria is thinking, "It was so hard to leave our oldest son, Tom, in college in the United States. We have always had such a special bond, and I have had to leave him on and off ever since he went to the Christian boarding school in the Philippines. Soon Stan and Julie will be nearing high school age, and I cannot even bear to think about being separated from them, too, as they will go to the boarding school in the Philippines. I never felt called to be a missionary. I just knew God wanted me to be Rob's wife, and Rob had the call. It is easier for him because he is of Chinese ancestry and blends in better. Even though I have Hispanic ancestry, I look very similar to the Chinese people physically, except for my eyes. I have to wear sunglasses so I will look Chinese, because people here are so hungry to talk to foreigners that with my sunglasses off people bombard me. I understand this because their government puts such blocks on any outside information that people just want to find out about the rest of the world. At first I felt flattered to be treated almost like a movie star, but now it has become most exhausting. As long as I keep my sunglasses on, I can pass for Chinese."

The first Chinese lady, Suli, is thinking, "I have heard that these people come from the United States and would be willing to talk about who God is. I don't know if I should let them talk to me or not. I have always believed in reincarnation and receiving the good and bad I did in my past life in the new earth life I flow into, whether it be person or animal, until finally I reach the god state of pure energy in the eternal peace and rest of nirvana. I believe that Jesus was a great ascended human spirit that is an example for us all as a place to reach toward, but I hear that they say he is something much more and different than this. I believe in praying and sacrificing food to my dead ancestors who may have reached the perfect place with Buddha instead of having to be reincarnated again. I may set up bad karma if I talk with them instead of placing myself on the path of good karma. Will I anger the spirit gods? But what if there is the possibility that God is much different from the way I have been taught. Wouldn't I want to know who he truly is? What should I do?"

The second Chinese lady, Maying, is thinking, "I heard that these people are religious. I side with my government in thinking that there is no religion. We are all just a result of evolutionary processes and even though there is a life force, it has nothing to do with a being who is a personal God. It is the here and now only that matters. When I die, I will turn back into dust and be gone. So I will try to improve the quality of my life now by accepting the medical help these people can give me, but if they try to shove any of that religious stuff on me, I will report them to the officials."

The third Chinese lady, Titi, is thinking, "I am a secret Christian, but I am afraid to let these people know. If they get in trouble, the worst that will happen to them and their family is that they will be deported back to their country. Whereas, if I get in trouble for making the officials mad with my religious beliefs, my family and I could be imprisoned, tortured, or killed. Who knows if Suli or Maying will tell on me to gain favors with the authorities?"

My daydream continues, soaring above the whole world, and I see people as dots. Some of them are lit up inside by God, scattered all over the earth. There are more people not lit up than those who are lit up. Some of the believers' lights are shining brightly and some are shining dimly, but anyone lit up is God's child.

I see God's Spirit whisper into some of his children's thoughts to pray for the missionaries and believers and God's working in China. Some people respond to the whispers and began fervently praying, and some do not respond.

Back in China, above the heads of the people in the room, I see an angel and a demon facing off. These angels are invisible to the humans on earth. Angels are made different than humans, even though they also have a spirit just like humans do. They have powers that earthly humans do not possess. Angels seem to be able to shape-shift into various projected forms. At times they can even shift their projected forms into our dimension so that people in the material world can see, hear, and touch them in their minds or with their senses. The angel, named Shimer, looks like a giant, strong man. His light skin keeps reflecting all the colors of the rainbow. He becomes mostly red, orange, yellow, green, blue, and purple as he turns. He has on a white robe over a white shirt and pants. He has sparkly silver hair in dreadlocks down his back. The demon, named Deger, keeps changing shapes, depending on how he is feeling. He starts off as a giant, muscular, light-skinned man dressed in a black leather coat and pants. He has black eyes, short black hair, a black mustache, and a black beard. He keeps changing skin colors. Then he starts to change into all different kinds of ferocious beasts that seem straight out of any of the most frightening science fiction movies.

Shimer and Deger both extend their arms up while still facing off, and a brilliant silver sword appears in both their hands. They begin to fight a fierce battle. They do not die during earth time, so they can't kill each other, but the wounds they inflict on each other cause pain and weakness. The angel and demon fly out of the room to the rooftops. They come back into the room and the people are unaware of their presence as they fight right through the people. They only connect with each other and each other's swords. The sparks fly and Deger seems to be winning while Shimer is losing energy.

Then the Christians around the world begin to pray and Shimer gains strength and the fight continues in the room, then through the ceiling to the sky, and back down to the busy street below. People on bicycles ride right through them, unaware of the intense struggle going on.

Finally Deger loses all his energy, and Shimer stands over Deger, who lies on a grassy patch under a tree, no strength left. Shimer takes Deger's sword and throws it to the sky where it dissipates, and soon Deger also fads away, floating toward an idol shrine so that he can regain his strength.

Shimer turns into a Chinese man and walks into Rob's office. Rob greets him and asks if he can do something to help. Shimer just tells him everything is going to be all right. Rob looks down at his desk while he asks Shimer if he can schedule an appointment for him. When Rob looks up, the man has disappeared, and Rob feels such a great peace in his heart from God. He asks himself if it could have been one of God's angels visiting him. Then he thinks he will never really truly know who the man was until he goes home to be with God.

Everyone else has been busy and hasn't seen the man.

The medical room in China is cleared of evil spirits and Shimer watchs happily as the Holy Spirit begins whispering in people's thoughts simultaneously. Maria looks at Rob and feels so much love for him. She thinks how fortunate she is to have married a man with so much love for God and people. She thinks about how blessed she is to have her three children who love being in China as much as being in the United States. They have beautiful hearts and minds, they have all become believers, and they are all healthy. What more can she want for her children?

Rob thinks about how his own father became a child of God on his last furlough. He prays for these three Chinese ladies to also open their hearts to God.

Suli and Titi think they might sneak back later when no one else is around just to hear what words these strangers may have to offer about God.

When Deger feels a little better he finds Satan and a lot of his buddies partying. Satan is enjoying the special mentoring relationship that is developing between himself and Deger. He takes Deger to a human party that is enjoying evil, where Deger gains so much pleasure and strength from people's sin that he is soon feeling like his old self again and is determined to destroy Shimer if they ever should meet again.

"Satan, I'm sorry I didn't beat Shimer."

"You tried your best. Rob and Maria are strong servants of God. I should have sent you with reinforcements."

"You know they were under the same pastor that Ted was under for a while. I really hate that pastor. We blew it with Ted also. Remember, it was right after the Vietnam War. Ted was that long-haired hippie that was into astral projection. We thought we could scare him into coming more deeply into our evil power by projecting our scary images into his mind on one of his trips; instead he called to God. Our enemy led him to one of that pastor's Bible studies. He turned traitor and brought his friends to that pastor's church and they all got saved. The church members treated them warmly instead of what we were hoping for. They became a powerful force on the wrong side and gave up a rocking lifestyle for complete boredom. I hate that pastor. It is hard staying one step ahead of God when he knows everything that is going to happen and he uses everything to flow into working toward the good for all his children. He uses evil to work his good will even though he hates evil. I'm glad I'm no longer one of his children. My will is my own. I choose to follow you, my liege."

"Don't worry about it. You took the opportunity to plant and encourage a lot of bad thoughts in all their minds that we may be able to take advantage of later."

"I wish we could read their thoughts and talk to people and they could talk to us all the time without any interference," sighed Deger.

"Deger, I am going to explain some things to you that some of my demon followers never really get. We have to have open doors in their minds and often the doors are closed, but there are a lot open here tonight. Would you like to pretend you are this woman's dead husband for this seance? You know our demon Sekhon? He is an enlightened angel like us. Sekhon was this woman's dead husband's personal demon spirit guide while he lived on this earth. He can feed you a lot of information that will make her believe you are the real thing because he was with the husband for most of his life. You can talk and shape-shift into their dimension like you are the dead husband for a bit. If you want to, you can even give one of the humans some body ailments that make them fear our power, and come to us for help, which we always make sure backfires on them in some way. You can even manipulate their material world and make some things float around for a while if you want to. The medium's ready for us to talk now. Would you like to do the honors?" Satan asked.

"Yes, thanks. This will definitely make me feel like getting back into the fight against God. Even though his power may be greater than ours, we have always been able to gain more of a human following than he has," Deger answered.

"Deger, I am considering moving you up in power. You may even get to be a principality prince over a whole nation if you get knowledgeable enough. Maybe you will even be a king god someday. As you know, all of us enlightened angels have different viewpoints and skill sets just like the humans do. The best fun we seem to have is interacting with humans for some reason. Everything else seems so much less boring than the challenge of keeping them on the evil side. Some of my demons actually think they are doing the people good by feeding them enlightened knowledge. We all tend to want to interact with the humans that are more like us I guess. Some of my demons just like to get as much possession of a person's soul and body as possible. Many have their pet sins that they enjoy and they follow families down generations to get high on that certain special sin that they can't get enough of as they feel the entrapped pleasure with their human host. A human's spirit is only reserved for God so we can't get in there, but the soul is attached so we can have a big influence to keep people in whatever dark they will buy into. This is the pleasure we share together. Someday we can all say that we did it my own way in hell before we are gone. Meantime we won't let some dictator control us just because he made us. If he didn't want us to use our free will, he shouldn't have given us one. I am leading people the better way any day. Unbelievers have a dead spirit like we do anyway, so who cares? Animals don't have a spirit, but they do have a soul and a body. My demons usually get more thrills from possessing a human, but a lot of my demons like to be directed into the soul and body of an animal or take the form of an animal to hang out with their special twisted person. Sometimes a bunch of them like to cram into one being. They hate when Jesus kicks them out when they have found a place where they can experience and promote evil to a greater degree and feel things they can't feel without human interactions. I am a better manager than God, but this makes me a better god because I let people and angels follow me into true freedom to do whatever evil they prefer. Some demons are just looking for an entrance into almost any living being; I'm much more picky about who I grant the privilege of joining me in possession. I hate God so much. I don't want to be his friend and I don't want anyone else to be his friend, because friendship with him is synonymous with robotic control. Being burned up and gone someday is worth having freedom for however long we can have it, even if I have to suffer some punishment before I go. And who knows? I might even defeat him in the end and then everyone would be instantly gone and no one would have to be punished at all. But even if I don't defeat him, this life disconnected from his chains is worth it. So what if I'm going to hell and taking as many with me as I can get? Everyone should thank me," Satan explained.

"I hear you and I get you, Master," Deger responded enthusiastically.

"I like your fighting spirit, Deger. I think you were meant to rule. Power is your evil of choice, just like me. You understand anything against the will of God is evil and you enjoy being on the road to hell and taking as many humans with you as possible instead of getting so distracted like many of my legions. Though if all of us demons defeat God at the last battle, we'll take over and avoid hell all together. Since, unfairly, God is the only one that wasn't created, we are almost guaranteed to lose. At least God is giving us a shot. I'm not sure what kind of shot it is since he knows every move we are going to make before we make it, and we have to stay within the boundaries of what we are allowed and not allowed to do or he will send us to hell's waiting room early. I don't like being tied to the human will any more than

I like being tied to God's will, I like the human will to follow me. This is all God gives me until his unfair judgment day, so I am going to get as wild as I can get. I'm more competitive than God realized since more people are following me into hell than following him into heaven. I love taking away all his possible friends. I hate him. He humiliated me and humiliates me. He thinks just because he created everyone and everything that he knows best how to rule. I disagree. I am rebellious as I can possibly be. I have to go give out assignments now. One of them has to do with inciting more very hidden ritual torture in a human occult group. I know you would like that one. I use my evil ways to bring people fame, fortune, money, power, popularity, dream fulfillment, sexual immorality, and anything else they may crave within their soul and body. I show people how to go against God's will to fulfill all of their desires. They use the way God created them in body and soul to work against him, just like I do. It is God's fault that the evil way always ends up so hurtful to everyone in the end. I am sharing my special insights with you because I am grooming you for much more. You are getting more powerful," Satan finished charismatically.

"Thank you, my Emperor Lord Satan, my first god among many gods. All of us demons are in the brotherhood with you and under you to do your bidding," said Deger, falling more and more under the spell of his magnificent master.

Steller and Jobber overhear the exchange, but do not participate in it. When it is over, they leave the party to go to the desert. The demons are dancing madly in the desert to a drumbeat in their heads. Day or night makes no difference to them as their spirits are given up to the distorted, electrifying excitement of complete anarchy.

Steller and Jobber sit on the sidelines and discuss things. They are dark, shape-shifting shadows. Since only demons inhabit this land, they can present themselves into the material world in whatever manner they like at the moment. Jobber looks like a goat man. He has huge horns, but he is careful not to present himself too much like one of the favorite shapes of his master. Even though his master encourages free expression, even he exerts subtle and not-so-subtle control over his minions. All the demons have felt the master's wrath at one time or another, and they much prefer to get back in his good graces as quickly as possible. Steller looks like a blue fairy, in the shape of a woman with a shimmering blue gown and wings and flowing white hair.

"It doesn't seem fair that God casts us into this place of only living vicariously through human hosts," Steller says.

"It is what it is. We have our memories intermixed with their memories and we have life on our own terms instead of God's terms," Jobber responds.

"Sometimes I actually regret thinking that they will be tortured and then burned away with us. I don't know if there is still some goodness in me as I try to help them with my white magic and humanism. Lies have become our truth," Steller says.

"I like experiencing sex with them, especially sex that God tells them is wrong. Even though it leads to misery, it is so electrifying while it lasts. Sometimes I try to influence adults to groom children so that when one human gets burned out on this, I can flip to the next one. I like them to feel emotionally that they were born to be deviant sexually. Why should they have to live in marital faithfulness or accept the gender identity that God assigned them? God even wants hermaphrodites to choose a side and stay within marital sexual boundaries. God seems to restrict freedom so much. Then we have to encourage them not to go back to God if their conscience rankles them because of the consequences. I think if God truly wanted people to have a free will, he wouldn't have given them, or us, a conscience, though I think I've pretty much eradicated my conscience by now. God says he will forgive any sin they commit and heal the harm that evil inflicts upon them. Is it harmful to live the way one desires without restraint? Then we either have to make them feel bad about going against their own conscience, or help them learn to block their conscience almost entirely.

"Deger, I don't know why God didn't give us bodies that can experience sex on our own without being involved emotionally with what they are doing. It is not fair that they can have children and we cannot. It is not fair that they are genetically linked and we are not. I would like to be able to have children, but God never gave us that ability like he gave to humans. The only children that I can have are the human spirits that I can influence. God is above sex and the unfallen angels experience this state with him, and humans will come to this state when they enter heaven, but sex on earth is so wild. God only allows humans to experience the best sex in a committed marriage, but we can keep the unfair consequences of having sex outside of marriage a secret, because evil sex is a blast and we can heighten this experience for all of us as we interact with them until their eventual bodily death, but then there are always more willing participants coming up. Since I can feel the feelings of people I am involved with I know this; even if I don't have a physical body that can feel what they feel, I can feel it in my soul. If abortions come through so-called sexual immorality, that is one less human that we have to worry about crossing over to God's side and being a shining light to God as they live on this earth. I don't even care that these aborted babies get to go right to heaven to be with God and won't share hell with us. The more humans who die, the less we have to worry about those who might shine a light on this earth. We are the rulers here and we don't like shining lights. By getting people to think no kind of sex is wrong, we can shut down religious influence by playing the victim card. Life can be so much fun, especially evil life," laughed Steller.

"You've got that right, Steller," Jobber answered. "After everything that has gone down, I have come to the place of hating God and hating any human who sides with him. We are the power of the air with our master. We are the pull of yin and yang that keeps the earth in balance with our good and bad magic. We are their gods. You were never destined to be a principality, as I believe I will be one day, but that doesn't mean that you can't have your fun as well. Just do your thing. You never know: our master may one day overcome God in the final battle, and then the universe will be ours."

"Steller, remember how we both worked that guy Steward together? That was so great. I made him so scared he cried, and he thought he was such a tough guy," chuckled Jobber.

"Then I came to him as twinkling dots of light and appeared to him as his grandmother's ghost and I patted his head and told him not to be afraid," reminisced Steller.

"That was great. Almost as good as when we trick people with our imaginations when they have near-death experiences. These humans are way too easy. Steward is, right now, in soul sleep, awaiting the judgment and then hell. So another one is ours. We get a lot more than God does right now. Good and bad, it is all the same: a balance to keep people away from God, the control freak. Anyway, what was your point?" asked Jobber.

"Sometimes I regret leaving God. I haven't felt real love since I left him, even though I have felt many things I know I could not have felt with him. Sometimes I feel bad keeping humans from God. Maybe this regret will give me less punishment in hell before I am completely burned away and gone after my judgment when I enter hell. Sometimes I look forward to being gone. We are more like the males in the human species, but we are spirits, without gender. The only sexual excitement or emotional sensations we seem able to experience is through getting a human host to open doors in their minds to our dwelling with them. Then it is almost like we have a human body like they do. I like to influence them psychologically, emotionally, and spiritually. At least we can trick them into opening doors of their soul for us so we can influence them. We like going down generational families and using all the tricks we can feed them through our knowledge of past events, because we actually lived through them. We can enter their thoughts and even enter their material dimension to a certain extent, depending on how much of their will they give to us. I am so bored here when I am not inhabiting them, but I wish I could have more pleasure without having to interact with them. I wonder when we are all in hell together if I will feel bad for leading them away from God," Steller said.

"You are being a drag," sighed Jobber. "I love torture, rape, death, destruction, addiction, abuse, and lunacy, and I love being a part in bringing it about and experiencing these things with them. The more my human host interacts with movies, drugs, art, fame, power, riches, music, porn, games, abuse, sexual immorality, power control, and social situations that lead to greater and greater evil, the more I feel a kinship and friendship with that human. Of course what God calls wrong, I call right and the exercising of freedom. I especially like to get involved with people who have sex with children, we can really mess with these children's minds and draw them into our world for a lifetime unless they let the Holy Spirit get involved. I love hanging with people drawn to evil; we are like soulmates. I feel bad when the evil eventually consumes and destroys them. It is a lot worse though if our enemy God gets a hold of them and I completely lose my influence and they start thinking and doing things that I can't stand. I let demons like you poke at and confuse religious people from time to time to try to make them less of an influence for God's side. I can't even stand being around them. We need all different types of us to target all the people, especially the children in the families, the churches, the schools, and the governments. You don't mind going to church and getting involved in their boring religious sins. Of course, we all have our pets for a time. I'm going to dance and go. Remember that we followed the master out of heaven to enjoy our lives anyway we choose, so enjoy it while you can," said Jobber with a flash, and then he was gone.

Steller turns into a tiger and runs through the starry night back to an orgy that is going on. Steller has an open door into a man that Steller knows. There are other friend demons with the man also and Steller feels better for the moment. The man has tried to leave the lifestyle, but has never become God's child, so now he is theirs to enjoy and Steller is going to use his influence to have pleasure any way he can until his time was up.

Isaiah 13:21: "But wild beasts of the desert shall lie there; and their houses shall be full of doleful creatures; and owls shall dwell there, and satyrs shall dance there."

PRAYERS AGAIN:

Dear God,
Is that sort of how it is?

Dear Christie,
Silver sparkling dreadlocks?

Dear God,
Creatures with wheels within wheels?

Ezekiel 28:11-19: "Moreover the word of the Lord came unto me, saying, 'Son of man, take up a lamentation upon the king of Tyrus, and say unto him. "Thus saith the Lord God; 'Thou sealest up the sum, full of wisdom, and perfect in beauty. Thou hast been in Eden the garden of God; every precious stone was thy covering, the sardius, topaz, and the diamond, the beryl, the onyx, and the jasper, the sapphire, the emerald, and the carbuncle, and gold; the workmanship of thy tabrets and of thy pipes was prepared in thee in the day that thou wast created. Thou art the anointed cherub that covereth; and I have set thee so; thou was upon the holy mountain of God; thou hast walked up and down in the midst of the stones of fire. Thou wast perfect in thy ways from the day that thou wast created, till iniquity was found in thee. By the multitude of thy merchandise they have filled the midst of thee with violence, and thou hast sinned; therefore I will cast thee as profane out of the mountain of God; and I will destroy thee, O covering cherub, from the midst of the stones of fire. Thine heart was lifted up because of thy beauty, thou hast corrupted thy wisdom by reason of thy brightness; I will cast thee to the ground, I will lay thee before kings, that they may behold thee. Thou hast defiled thy sanctuaries by the multitude of thy traffic; therefore will I bring forth a fire from the midst of thee, it shall devour thee, and I will bring thee to ashes upon the earth in the sight of all them that behold thee. All they that know thee among the people shall be astonished at thee; thou shalt be a terror, and never shalt thou be any more.'"''

Daniel 10:10-21: "And behold, a hand touched me, which set me upon my knees and upon the palms of my hands. And he said unto me, 'O Daniel, a man greatly beloved, understand the words that I speak unto thee, and stand upright; for unto thee am I now sent.' And when he had spoken this word unto me, I stood trembling. Then said he unto me, 'Fear not, Daniel; for from the first day that thou didst set thine heart to understand, and to chasten thyself before thy God, thy words were heard, and I am come for thy words. But the prince of the kingdom of Persia withstood me one and twenty days; but, lo, Michael, one of the chief princes, came to help me; and I remained there with the kings of Persia. Now I am come to make thee understand what shall befall thy people in the latter days; for yet the vision is for many days.' And when he had spoken such words unto me, I set my face toward the ground, and I became dumb. And, behold, one like the similitude of the sons of men touched my lips; then I opened my mouth, and spake, and said unto him that stood before me, 'O my lord, by the vision my sorrows are turned upon me, and I have retained no strength. For how can the servant of this my lord talk with this my lord? For as for me, straightway there remained no strength in me, neither is there breath left in me.' Then there came again and touched me one like the appearance of a man, and he strengthened me, and said, 'O man greatly beloved, fear not; peace be unto thee, be strong, yea, be strong.' And when he had spoken unto me, I was strengthened, and said, 'Let my lord speak; for thou hast strengthened me.' Then said he, 'Knowest thou wherefore I come unto thee? And now will I return to fight with the prince of Persia; and when I am gone forth, lo, the prince of Grecia shall come. But I will shew thee that which is noted in the Scripture of truth; and there is none that holdeth with me in these things, but Michael your prince.'"

Dear God,
It seems like fallen angels often try to convince people that there is no you, or that you are very different than you are, or that having any kind of connection with you is an impossible dream.

Mark 5:7-8: "And cried with a loud voice, and said, 'What have I to do with thee, Jesus, thou Son of the most high God? I adjure thee by God, that thou torment me not.' For he said unto him, 'Come out of the man, thou unclean spirit.'"

Luke 9:23-25: "And he said to them all, 'If any man will come after me, let him deny himself, and take up his cross daily, and follow me. For whosoever will save his life shall lose it; but whosoever will lose his life for my sake, the same shall save it.'"

John 8:36: "If the Son therefore shall make you free, ye shall be free indeed."

Matthew 6:14-15: "For if ye forgive men their trespasses, your heavenly Father will also forgive you: But if ye forgive not men their trespasses, neither will your Father forgive your tresspasses."

Matthew 7:1-2: "Judge not, that ye be not judged, for with what judgment ye judge, ye shall be judged; and with what measure ye mete, it shall be measured to you again."

John 8:44: "Ye are of your Father the devil, and the lusts of your father ye will do. He was a murderer from the beginning, and abode not in the truth, because there is no truth in him. When he speaketh a lie, he speaketh of his own; for he is a liar, and the father of it."

First Corinthians 3:1-2: "And I, brethren, could not speak unto you as unto spiritual, but as unto carnal, even as unto babes in Christ. I have fed you with milk, and not with meat; for hitherto ye were not able to bear it, neither yet now are ye able."

First John 2:16–17: "For all that is in the world, the lust of the flesh, and the lust of the eyes, and the pride of life, is not of the Father, but is of the world. And the world passeth away, and the lust thereof; but he that doeth the will of God abideth forever."

Isaiah 14:14: "I will ascend above the heights of the clouds; I will be like the Most High."

Revelation 20:10: "And the devil that deceived them was cast into the lake of fire and brimstone, where the beast and the false prophet are, and shall be tormented day and night for ever and ever."

Ephesians 6:10–18: "Finally, my brethren, be strong in the Lord, and in the power of his might. Put on the whole armour of God, that ye may be able to stand against the wiles of the devil. For we wrestle not against flesh and blood, but against principalities, against powers, against the rulers of the darkness of this world, against spiritual wickedness in high places. Wherefore take unto you the whole armour of God, that ye may be able to withstand in the evil day, and having done all, to stand. Stand therefore, having your loins girt about with truth, and having on the breastplate of righteousness; and your feet shod with the preparation of the gospel of peace; above all, taking the shield of faith, wherewith ye shall be able to quench all the fiery darts of the wicked. And take the helmet of salvation, and the sword of the Spirit, which is the word of God; praying always with all prayer and supplication in the Spirit, and watching thereunto with all perseverance and supplication for all saints."

Second Corinthians 10:4–5: "For the weapons of our warfare are not carnal, but mighty through God to the pulling down of strong holds; casting down imaginations, and every high thing that exalteth itself against the knowledge of God, and bringing every thought to the obedience of Christ."

Second Corinthians 2:11: "Lest Satan should get an advantage of us: for we are not ignorant of his devices."

Deuteronomy 9:4: "Speak not thou in thine heart, after that the Lord thy God hath cast them out from before thee, saying for my righteousness, or for the uprightness of thine heart, doest thou go to possess their land; but for the wickedness of these nations the Lord thy God doth drive them out from before thee, and that he may perform the word which the lord sware unto thy fathers, Abraham, Isaac, and Jacob."

Romans 4:3–5: "For what saith the Scripture? Abraham believed God, and it was counted unto him for righteousness. Now to him that worketh is the reward not reckoned of grace, but of debt. But to him that worketh not, but believeth on him that justifieth the ungodly, his faith is counted for righteousness."

Isaiah 14:12–15: "How art thou fallen from heaven, O Lucifer, son of the morning! How art thou cut down to the ground, which didst weaken the nations! For thou hast said in thine heart, 'I will ascend into heaven, I will exalt my throne above the stars of God; I will sit also upon the mount of the congregation, in the sides of the north; I will ascend above the heights of the clouds; I will be like the Most High.' Yet thou shalt be brought down to hell, to the sides of the pit."

Revelation 12:4: "And his tail drew the third part of the stars of heaven, and did cast them to the earth; and the dragon stood before the woman which was ready to be delivered, for to devour her child as soon as it was born."

Revelation 12:7–9: "And there was war in heaven; Michael and his angels fought against the dragon; and the dragon fought and his angels. And prevailed not; neither was their place found any more in heaven. And the great dragon was cast out, that old serpent, called the Devil, and Satan, which deceiveth the whole world: he was cast out into the earth, and his angels were cast out with him."

Dear Christie,

I am very different from angels or people. My Bible reveals the truth about me. I am absolutely self-sufficient (Acts 17:25). I am absolutely immortal and eternal (Ps 90:2; Isa 40:28). I am the only being not created and I create and sustain all things (Acts 17:25–28; Heb 1:3; Ps 33:6–9). I am all-powerful (Jer 32:17). I can be known, but never fully known (Isa 40:28). I know everything (Rom 16:27 and Dan 2:21). I am three persons in one (1 John 5:7). I am everywhere (Ps 139:8). I am completely good and holy (Rom 11:22; 1 Sam 2:2; Isa 6:3). I am a Spirit (John 4:24). I am present everywhere that I want to be (Ps 139:7–12). I am absolute truth (Heb 6:8; John 4:6). I am absolute love, mercy, and graciousness (Luke 6:36; 1 John 4:7–8; 1 Pet 2:2–3). I am the ultimate judge of all spirit beings (Jas 4:12). The core of who I am will never change (Jas 1:17).

Dear God,

I know that even fallen angels will not cross the boundaries that you have for them, because they are afraid that you will put them in prison instead of letting them interact with humans.

Second Peter 2:4: "For if God spared not the angels that sinned, but cast them down to hell, and delivered them into chains of darkness, to be reserved unto judgment."

Second Corinthians 10:5: "Casting down imaginations, and every high thing that exalteth itself against the knowledge of God, and bringing into captivity every thought to the obedience of Christ."

Dear God,
I'm not sure how much I am getting wrong or right about demons, but I am going to present you with what I think I know from my life journey with you. These entities are invisible to me, and since I am on your side and they are your enemies they are my enemies also. I know you love everyone, even them, you grieve that they left you. You grieve for any people who follow them away from you. You cry inside that any fallen angel or human is destined for hell, to be forever separated from you and the eternal life they could have had with you. Your love and care is what makes you so angry at fallen angels or people allowing the pull of evil and sin to influence them. It seems that sometimes fallen angels or people get pulled into evil to such an extent that you have to take them out of earth's picture in a type of partial judgment before the final judgment.

I'm guessing that people influenced by demons can intentionally or unintentionally help other people to also form links with demons. Demmons can travel down generational lines in a family, jumping into the life of a younger family member when an older family member dies, or bringing friend demons to influence other family members. Some demons are more wicked or powerful than other demons. People can be strongly pulled toward specific sins; sometimes it is because the same demon has open doors to influence a family for generations. Spiritual leaders that connect people to fallen angels may be shamans, wizards, musicians, writers, actors, artists, warlocks, witches, voodoo people, spell-casters, psychics, wiccans, witch doctors, false priests, false prophets, demonically influenced political leaders, false religious leaders, new age humanists, demonically influenced people of power and money, fortune-tellers, healers, monks and others that teach reincarnation and/or false beliefs, and any leader that heals or grants wishes apart from submission to you. They can appear to be good or evil. They themselves may think they are benevolent or malevolent toward people, but any interactions that people have with them always hurt, because they can never be you or lead people toward finding you.

I'm guessing that Satan lets demons choose how they want to lead people into being their own gods since demons have personalities, skill sets, and interests. Demons can interact with people in a so-called good way or bad way, but either way will be a circular spiral toward the second death instead of finding real life in connection to you, the one and only true, immortal, omniscient, omnipotent, eternal, loving, and just God. We will never find the reason we were made if we don't find a connection to you.

I'm guessing that demons can influence people to worship Satan or to become witches, psychics, illuminati, warlocks, wiccans, or whatever else has contact with the so-called force of the universe. They often use stories and games to draw people into their world. Demons can appear to use their wisdom mostly for enlightenment, good, healing, success, wealth, fame, and power, but the dark side will infect the person's life.

When I surrender to the real you, I feel your love and hear your voice and see you do amazing works. When I let anyone, anything, or any thought take your place because I don't want to surrender to you, either because I am afraid or I want my own way, or I think I know better than you, or I don't want to wait on you, or I think the material is more important than your Spirit, beautiful things do not happen. I get stuck in a dark place internally, until I finally surrender to your will and let you do amazing things in my life and in other people's lives. A lot of Christians in history have really messed up trying to do your will without the guidance of your Spirit. As I surrender and don't surrender to the leading of your Spirit and step out before I see what the future will bring, I am learning that your will is always best and it makes me free inside instead of in bondage, no matter what my outward circumstances are on the outside.

Second Corinthians 5:7: "For we walk by faith, not by sight."

John 4:24: "God is spirit; and they that worship him must worship him in spirit and in truth.

Ephesians 6:10–18: "Finally, my brethren, be strong in the Lord, and in the power of his might. Put on the whole armour of God, that ye may be able to stand against the wiles of the devil. For we wrestle not against flesh and blood, but against principalities, against powers, against the rulers of the darkness of this world, against spiritual wickedness in high places. Wherefore take unto you the whole armour of God, that ye may be able to withstand in the evil day, and having done all, to stand. Stand therefore, having your loins girt about with truth, and having on the breastplate of righteousness; And your feet shod with the preparation of the gospel of peace; above all, taking the shield of faith, wherewith ye shall be able to quench all the fiery darts of the wicked. And take the helmet of salvation, and the sword of the Spirit, which is the word of God; praying always with all prayer and supplication in the Spirit, and watching thereunto with all perseverance and supplication for all saints."

Second Peter 3:9: "The Lord is not slack concerning his promise, as some men count slackness; but is longsuffering to usward, not willing that any should perish, but that all should come to repentance."

Dear God,

Every human is born lost to you in sin and your Spirit draws every human toward you so that you can find them and make them your own. Every human is born with a free will, but you know who will become yours and who won't become yours. Even though you never take away any human's free choice and your Spirit calls to each human to come to you, you interact with humans based on the knowledge you have of the choice they will make for or against you and you incorporate it all into your plan. You never disown backslidden Christians, but they miss out on seeing what a spectacular friend you are on this earth.

Romans 9:20-23: "Nay, but, O man, who art thou that repliest against God? Shall the thing formed say to him that formed it, 'Why hast thou made me thus?' Hath not the potter power over the clay, of the same lump to make one vessel unto honour, and another unto dishonour? What if God, willing to shew his wrath, and to make his power known, endured with much longsuffering the vessels of wrath fitted to destruction; and that he might make known the riches of his glory on the vessels of mercy, which he had afore prepared unto glory."

Luke 19:10: "For the Son of man is come to seek and to save that which was lost."

Dear Christie,

If you want to talk about hell, we will talk about hell later on in this prayer journal you are writing.

Dear God,
Thank you.

Dear God,

Here is a letter I wrote to my son, Ricky, trying to try to explain the spiritual battle of good and evil going on in this world. I feel like his generation is going to be under an intense spiritual struggle, but you are there for every generation and each of your children.

Dear Ricky,

Evil is like this dark blob of darkness with octopus-like tentacles that is directed by the powerful mind of Satan, who supervises the fallen angels.

The whole purpose for a human's earthly existence is to find and link their spirit to the God who created them. The Messiah made this possible. If Satan can't keep a human from linking up to be part of God's family, then he will try to keep them as isolated from God as possible. Satan hates God, and he hates humans because they were made in the image of God. God loves everyone and is very sad that Satan chose to lve for evil. God knew this door to evil would have to be opened when he created sentient beings to have a love relationship with. The only two types of sentient beings that we know that God created are angels and humans.

God is out of time and space, but when a human personally invites God into their spirit, God comes into their time and space to communicate with that person. Then that person starts to have the wisdom of God, who is out of time and space.

Adam and Eve were made with spirits that were alive to God. Their bodies never would have died if they had not opened the door for evil for all people. However, God did not make them immortal. When they opened the door to evil, they did not die immediately, but they were on their way to dying unless they received the redemption that God gave at great cost to himself. Their bodies began to decay and would eventually experience the first death. And while Adam and Eve lost that spirit link to God, no one else who links their spirit to God can lose that link. Hell was made to burn up the fallen angels after they had paid whatever price that judgment dictated for them, but now unbelieving humans also go there.

God offered Adam and Eve, and every human throughout history, a way to redeem their spirit and soul so that they never have to experience the second death. God knew what it would take the Messiah to do this and he did it. When a person comes to God in faith and repentance, their spirit and soul is forever linked to God, Jesus, and the Holy Spirit, and only then are they sealed to be given immortality and eternal life. Their spirit and soul will never die, and they will eventually be given an immortal body to go with this. They never become annihilated or turn into anyone other than the unique being God created them as, but when their spirit leaves their body, the pull of sin is gone and the link to God is so strong that their perspective and wisdom continues growing with God, unfettered. A person could link their spirit to God before the Messiah died or after the Messiah died, because when God promised the Messiah his word would never be broken. That person who comes to God in repentance and faith acknowledges that no one except God has the power to deal with the evil that indwells them, because only God is great enough to overcome evil with good. Since God is out of time and space, his prophecies in the Bible about when the Messiah would bodily visit earth and do what he needed to do and how he needed to do it are not spoken of in a linear timeline in the Bible. This could cause confusion in people about the Messiah if they don't listen to the Spirit's voice for explanations. Also, the various metamorphoses that God's human believing children would and will go through as they journey with him often seemed jumbled in time, as he alludes to these throughout the Bible. Sometimes it can get very confusing to try to understand world history, past, present, and future, since each human enters the earthly linear timeline at a certain time and place, without a clear understanding of what came before and what will come afterward.

Genesis 3:2–5: "And the woman said unto the serpent, 'We may eat of the fruit of the trees of the garden; but of the fruit of the tree which is in the midst of the garden, God hath said, "Ye shall not eat of it, neither shall ye touch it, lest ye die."' And the serpent said unto the woman, 'Ye shall not surely die; for God doth know that in the day ye eat thereof, then your eyes shall be opened, and ye shall be as gods, knowing good and evil.'"

The human soul has the capacity to find God, even before their spirit has been made alive. Once a human spirit is made alive, God seeks to reveal to his child how every part of their life perceptions flow back to his love connection with them. God always wants his believers to make the jump from just obeying his laws because they want to get some kind of points, to obeying him because of the deep love and trust they have developed and are continuing to develop with him.

In the time and place that you and I are in, God mostly uses the written Bible to communicate personally to us with his Spirit. He takes the stories and lessons given to people in different times and places in history and makes it relevant to us, helping us right at the time and place we are in, sort of like God-magic. That's why we need to meditate on the Bible and open our minds to God in prayer every day if we can. God also speaks to us in our thoughts and in open and closed doors as we try to step out in his will, and he gives peace to our hearts to help us know that we are following his ways.

God asks that human sentient beings form an unbroken love bond with him. In forming this, they realize that they can only achieve true freedom by becoming God's willing slaves. Slavery to a human or fallen angel master puts a human in a place where they become trapped in a state of fighting nothingness and being without freedom. Willing slavery to God is the only way for an angel or human to obtain true freedom and self-actualization, which is an oxymoron.

Fallen and unfallen angels have more power than humans on earth, but no one and nothing ever has or will have more power than God. Fallen angels seem to be able to live without dying until after the final judgment when God consumes them in the fires of hell after their punishment is complete. They seem to live in a dimension that is mostly invisible to humans. However, the fallen angels can feed into a human's thought process that is open to them. They seem to be able to shape-shift sometimes and appear to humans in various forms, either in the realm of the human's mind or in the material realm. They can manipulate matter when doors are open to them, yet they still are subject to the boundaries God put in a place. If they cross these boundaries, they will have to wait in jail cells until the final judgment instead of enjoying evil with Satan. Their major enjoyment seems to come from getting humans to follow their influence. They are very bored when they are not manipulating humans.

They live through generations of humans and can plague generations in a family to follow the same sin through doors that were opened by their ancestors. At any time, a human can close that door by asking God's power to help them close it.

When an earthly believer becomes God's child, God synergistically links his spirit to their spirit. The spirit within an angel or human is what enables God to make that link with them. The earthly human just has to come to God, admitting that they are lost. They need to repent of their personal sin so that the Messiah has power to forever take away their punishment for all their sin—past, present, and future. Only then does God link his spirit to theirs in a forever-love bond. They walk into his kingdom as his own children and they are given eternal life. The unfallen angels are given immortality because they chose to never leave God.

Once a human is a believer, God wants them to form a close relationship with him partly so that they will shine as lights to other humans to come out of the evil's darkness and find and link to the one true God. Using earthly humans in his fight against evil is an exciting privilege and God knows how to use each one in a way that lights them up inside while they are being used.

Satan wants to stop a believer's light from shining, to block anyone that they might influence. One of the major ways he does this is through religion. If he can make a believer forget that only God can fit all the pieces of the puzzle together, then he can make that believer feel alone and disconnected from God, even though God never disconnects from any human once they become his child. Instead of listening to the voice of God as he walks with them through the earthly journey he has them on, they start hearing that they will never follow enough religious rules for God to even like them. They start pushing themselves and others to follow their idea of perfectionism to get God to like them or because they mistakenly believe that God needs their help to save them, and they lose the joy of intimacy with God. I fell into this trap for many years, and I hope and pray that you stay out of it.

God knows and loves you better than you know or love yourself. God always loves and forgives you. He tries to get you out of sin's traps when you fall in. He helps you through whatever valleys and storms your earthly journey brings you to in such a way that you grow deeper and deeper in wisdom and love with him, yourself, and others.

There seems to be two times in the life of a human where they question everything. The first time is usually sometime before a person enters either their career or gets married. This often happens sometime during the later teenage to young adult years. The second time is often called the mid-life crisis. This second time is usually sometime before or after retirement, and could hit people at different times. God planned for these times so that people would become stronger, wiser, and closer in him. He wants to help them stop and discern more of the deceptions that they may have entered into, so that they can come closer to God and his truth. Satan, of course, wants to use these times to totally derail a person. I pray for you as you are going through this first time.

No one can completely separate truth from fantasy while they are on this earth, but the more of God's truth that enters into us, the more we will know how to go into the garden to fellowship with God. I call this place of intimacy the garden because we can walk in and out of it, but from the first time we enter it with God, we always know from then on that the garden exists and we can get back to it. The garden is a place of joyous, loving, intimate friendship with God and surrender to God. It is a place that is not affected by any good or bad circumstances that we may be in while we travel on our earthly journey. It is the best place to be in the universe at any time. It is a place where we know that God is real, and that he is good, and that he loves us. It is a place where we hear his guidance in our thoughts.

It is a place where we talk to God and he talks back to us in our thoughts. It is a place of fun, insight, adventure, love, and purpose. It is a place where we know that all evil will eventually be overcome and only love and goodness will reign. It is a place where we let go of the fears that lies can bring in. When we let God's love and forgiveness and kindness flow through us, it comes back to us. God's love and goodness make us loving with God, ourselves, and others. God's love and goodness make us always lit up inside as we are close with him in his forever kingdom family.

Love,
Mom

PRAYERS AGAIN:

Dear God,
I can think of three times that I may have seen fallen and unfallen angels, but even these times are hard to be sure of. One time, when my car broke down in the middle of an intersection when Ryan was about three, I ran Ryan over to the sidewalk and told him to stay on the corner sidewalk, and then I ran to push my car out of the way. Suddenly about ten men of varying races came running over. They were dressed as homeless men. They pushed my car across the intersection into a parking lot. As they were doing this, I ran back to get Ryan before he could step out and get hit. I turned to look for the men to thank them and they had disappeared.

The next time I feel like I had an encounter was about two years ago, after Barry had just come out of his triple bypass surgery. I had stepped out of the room into the hallway as they were pulling the tube out of his throat. I felt very overwhelmed and frightened. A young man stood beside me in a doctor's coat. He had light skin and light brown hair. He was attractive in a caring kind of way. He asked me how it was going. I told him they were pulling the tube out of my husband's throat. He told me that everything would be all right. I looked at him and I felt such a peace, like he was very closely connected with you. I turned around and back again and he was gone.

One day, there was a little girl in my class who was exhibiting some strange behaviors that I tried to talk to her parents about. That same night, I saw a large, shadowy, menacing figure in my dream. I lost my job for trying to do the right thing and address the situation to help the student get better. The student's father had a lot of financial power in the church and I never made that much money in any job again, but I tried to follow you. I was teaching second grade at the time. I felt the little girl's heart calling out to my heart for me to help her. So I told the parents that their little girl had said her little friend, that was a boy, at school had touched her private area and she had touched his private area. I told the parents that some of the boys in the class had tattled on the little girl and said that she had grabbed their privates, but she had always said that she hadn't. No one had tattled on the boy like this. I showed the parents a picture she had drawn of boys and girls with their privates exposed. I wondered why the little girl had mentioned suicide, which the mother knew about, and why she had never told her parents these things about touching privates that she had told me. I wondered why the parents responded by attacking me, the school, the church, the boy, and didn't seem to want to really find out what was going on and try to help their daughter. The church and their church school was about to move to a bigger building in a better location and I guess the pastor handled the stress by letting the girl's father and me go at the end of the school year. I pray that God helps the girl since I never found out the rest of the story, and I pray that God blesses the ministry and I don't ever talk them down because no one can see things perfectly, but I never want to be involved myself with that ministry again because they didn't back me up. I am sure spiritual warfare was going on in the church, school, and in our homes, but I know you worked all things out for your good purposes like you always do. I went down very far inside to a place where I felt I lost my communication with everyone, including you and myself, but you brought me up to a better, wiser, and stronger place inside. Demons can be so confusing, but your power is so much stronger.

Hebrews 13:1–2: "Let brotherly love continue. Be not forgetful to entertain strangers; for thereby some have entertained angels unawares."

Hebrews 1:14: "Are thy not all ministering spirits, sent forth to minister for them who shall be heirs of salvation?"

Matthew 16:23: "But he turned, and said unto Peter, 'Get thee behind me, Satan; thou art an offence unto me; for thou savourest not the things that be of God, but those that be of men.'"

Chapter Three

Love Implosion

LITTLE MISS PERFECTION

    I'm little Miss Perfect, watch me perform.
    There will never be a need for me to reform.
    I'm the Christian church, correct in everything I do.
    You will never know if I ever get blue.
    My mommy and daddy are church leaders and I have to be good.
    I always have to be positive, just like a good girl should.
    Every thought and emotion is monitored before it comes out.
    Sometimes I'm so tense, all I want to do is shout.
    But my program says no.
    I'm not authentic, all I am is a robot, you know.
    I have no idea who I really am deep inside.
    Any true emotions, my religion cannot abide.
    Does anyone know how I feel as I try to do what I should?
    I try so hard to please everyone and always be good.
    Sometimes I dream of dancing, but my religion says all dancing is wrong.
    Sometimes I dream of music, but my religion says I'm listening to the wrong song,
    Sometimes I dream of laughing, but my religion says I laugh at the wrong time.

Sometimes I dream of poems, but my religion says be careful what human emotions you express in rhyme.
Sometimes I dream of playing, but my religion says this is not a wise way to spend my time.
I feel isolated and alone as I try to do what I think I should.
I want God to lead me instead of striving for others and myself, to always reflect respected religious people's ideas of good.
Am I here to be a religious image and a showpiece instead of being the real me?
I wonder why God said to worship him in truth and be free?
I wonder why God took so much trouble to create all humans in such a different and unique way?
Did God really want church to be a place where we will all strive to be proper Christian clones for yet another day?
I guess instead of knowing religious bents, I need to learn to know the God who loves me.
Even if I deviate from my religion's perfection, only God's true love can help me be the person I really want to be.
Only a synergistic love relationship with God can make me authentic and free.
How can I learn to consistently be able to hear God's voice and guiding will for me?

COLLEGE CONTEMPLATION

Is my existence worth anything, and do people look at me well?
The question continues to circle around my mind.
It causes me to plan and plot and in the uncertain future to dwell.
I frustratingly continue seeking some magic formulas for myself and others to find.
I try to make the right decisions, figuring my decisions will control my future life.
Then I pound my fist when circumstances envelop me with something my mind cannot fathom or I did not plan on.
As life continues, I see sin, sickness, suffering, and strife.
I begin to feel less powerful and more like a pawn.
Truth seems to fade into relativity as philosophies abound.
Are there absolutes where truth never bends?
Is there any plan I am in that can be found?
I see a lot of confusion in people, even in my close friends.

As I fling my questions, the answers are ambiguous and many, as people continue to expound unintentional lies.
There is no light and everything is dim.
I see things around me from the perspective of my own eyes.
Yet, doesn't truth in its purest sense stand unencumbered by anyone's conception of what seems wise to him?
It is hard to know the truth because of my earthly limitations and visional size.
None of this changes the factualness of truth and I need to trust God so that he can lead me to understand with his wisest mind.
God tells about all the world kingdoms that would come before they came and he tells about the last world government where he will reign as king.
There is ultimate truth in Jesus for me to find.
Keeping my eyes off the world and on God will make my heart continue to sing.
When I get off track God is great enough to get me back on track.
He can even use all the mistakes that others and myself made and make in my life.
God can work everything in my life into good and he always has my back.
Deep down I can lay down my fears, even in the midst of life's strife.

PATAGONIAN BALONEY

The world popped into existence all by itself from chemicals that were just always here.
There is no one out there creating or directing things, so we have no one we must be accountable to or love or worship or fear.
The design and function of the solar systems all came by chance through many years.
Species adapted and changed into other species, although we can't prove this because no fossil or other evidence appears.
Over time, a creature crawled out of the sea because he had decided to be a worm and breathe air.
The creature's name was Patagonian Baloney, and it had no hair. It crawled around for millions of years and began to decide things it would like or not like to be and pass on before it died.
As I tell you these deep truths of the past I wasn't present at, you are scientifically stupid if you say I lied.

Aren't you excited to be such an awesome animal, now having evolved yourself to the top of the animal world?
You're special, even if you decided against having wings and common sense and a few other things other animals have, because you are the ultimate, you are Patagonian Baloney unfurled.

RACES

At the beginning, people probably looked more similar and their language was the same.
Then one day, the Tower of Babel came.
People worked together for a bad cause.
They didn't want to obey God or his laws.
They wanted to build a high tower to dethrone God.
They forgot God created the original people they all descended from out of sod.
God knew they couldn't reach him.
But he didn't like their sin.
God decided that if people couldn't work together to follow his good, he would then divide.
God made each group speak a different language, so people decided to in their own group reside.
Each group went their separate ways, and those who didn't speak their language or look like their group were often scorned.
Each group's appearance must have changed to match their group, and this is probably when races were first formed.
God made people different shades of brown to reflect the earth color so their skin could reflect what he had used to make them.
Many people decided to only call people of their own race friends.
The tower was never finished, and now people often fight with God and each other.
God just wanted an opportunity for all people to become true sisters and brothers.
He wanted to give people a choice to find him and a love that is true.
These people will find ways to overcome racial obstacles because they love Jesus the Jew.
God picked the Hebrew race to be an example to all people to reveal the true God and his ways.
Sometimes the Hebrew race got it right and sometimes they got it wrong as they lived out their days.

One of the Three Persons of the one Triune God, called Jesus, the Messiah, came to earth as a perfect God-man to die and to take away the second death for any person who will make Jesus their own.
Even though people are linked into hell through sin passed through Adam, they could link to Jesus and gain heaven unless they choose their Savior to disown.
God made this world as a test, with obstacles that he picked.
God was hoping that each person would not get tricked.
Sin and the devil and free choice exist.
If the devil and people had succeeded in killing Jesus permanently, they would have killed God, and they themselves and everything would have ceased to exist.
Anything against God is ultimately self-destructive.
So, if people ever learn to work together again, hopefully, it will be more constructive.
The races may be different, but God never said one race was superior.
All people originated with Adam and Eve and no race is inferior.
Just because people are human doesn't mean they belong to the family of God.
Because humans are made in God's image, they can choose to enter God's family because they love him, even knowing that sometimes God has to teach and nudge us with his love rod.
This time of earth is a time to choose to get on God's side, to pass through evil to good.
God now uses his church, made of every race, like he used and uses the Hebrews to show the example of connecting to God the way he desires that all humans should.

RACISM IMPOSSIBILITY

Having taught every race of child in my classroom for so many years, I have been left with an inability to think badly of an entire race when negative things happen racially.
As soon as a negative thought comes into my mind about any race of people, a loving, intelligent, and beautiful child's face from that race of people comes into my mind.
For one year that child was mine and I was theirs and nothing can change the loving memories from that time.

Someday every race will joyfully share heaven together since God made all people in his image to become his own eternal beloved children.

DENOMINATIONAL DIFFERENCES

I've met true believers from every Christian denominational church.
We may have different interpretations of the Bible, but we all believe that the only way to become God's child is to repent and receive the payment Jesus provided.
Maybe God is like a diamond and we each see different facets of his beauty as we try to find the purposes God has for each of us on our long life's search.
When we are all in heaven together, maybe God's Spirit will explain why he gave differing truths of himself to different denominations as he confided.
One denomination saw more of God's feeling, one saw more of his tradition, one saw more of his doctrine, one saw more of his charity, one saw more of his leadership, one saw more of his healing, one saw more of his friendship, one saw more of his knowledge, and one saw more of his inner voice.
When God's whole warrior body is together under its head, then we will see more completely all of God's invisible power of overcoming evil with good throughout all of earth's history, and we will all rejoice.

Dear God,
Why can't you physically put your arms around me and hold me like my daddy did when I was a little girl? Why can't Jesus appear to me in physical form and talk with me and comfort me. I'm so lonely. I need you so much. I feel so alone.

Dear Christie,
I am a wise and loving counselor who can heal your emotional soul, your body, and your spirit. Talk to me. Let me help you. I'm with you. Talk with me.

Dear God,
Here is a memory I have of my dad and me from when I was a child.

"Daddy's home."

"I love you, Daddy," I say to my Father as I fling my five-year-old self into his arms when he comes in the door after work.

"Come to Daddy, Crissy. Sit on my lap and I will rock you and tell you a story. I will play my harmonica for you for special effects."

"Daddy, will you tell me the continuing story about the adventures of the black jewelry box you got for me last Christmas? You know, the one that has the hidden treasure in it that everyone is trying to get."

"Let's see, there was a mystery message and a hidden compartment with jewels in the mysterious black jewelry box hidden inside, and the little girl who owned it had no idea."

"Was the little girl named Crissy? Was it me, Daddy?"

"Yes, honey, she had golden curly hair and big brown eyes. Her name was Crissy, and she was you."

I was about five as I snuggled on my dad's lap and put my arms around him as he rocked me and told me the story and played his harmonica.

I felt such love and happiness at times like this, rocking with my dad as my mom finished making one of her delicious suppers. My parents helped to open my heart to give and receive love. My dad showed me the best way to point a child in your direction, God, which is to lovingly and creatively interact with the heart of a child, letting your love flow from your heart through our heart to their heart and back again.

When I grew up, I became a disappointment to my father in so many ways and our love became blocked. He wasn't happy that I was trying to work through some issues my mom and I had. He was right that I was going about trying to work out these issues in the wrong way.

My dad was also disappointed that I married Barry instead of a strong leader in his denomination. My dad was right that I married a very immature man, but my dad didn't understand how your love drew Barry and I together to help us both grow more mature. Barry came from a very poor and worldly home. He became a believer when he was sixteen and I met him when he was seventeen and I was nineteen. We wisely listened to my dad's advice to wait until Barry had gotten his General Equivalency High School Diploma and turned twenty before we got married. We couldn't keep our hands off each other and even though we petted a lot we waited to have sex until we got married because we were your children. His family often moved back and forth from Indiana to Florida, and when his family just left him in Florida when he was seventeen as they moved back to Indiana, my mother helped him get a job and an apartment, and she often invited him to share family meals and gave him motherly advice. Barry has always had a job even though he started off making little money until he got his air conditioner repair degree at the junior college across the street, and then his salary doubled. Meanwhile, I always worked as a teacher in Christian schools, so we needed each other's help financially, and in every other way, to make it in life. I always hoped Barry would become a really strong and mature Christian so I could prove to my dad that I didn't just marry him because I thought we would have good sex together, but Barry has mostly always been a baby Christian. Though we have enjoyed our sex life, it would have been nice to have had spiritual fellowship as well as the other things though. We never felt you were telling us not to get married and we still love each other after forty-some years, so I guess that is a lot. Even though our marriage has never reached the highest place of intimacy that marriage can reach, you have used it to give us two beautiful sons and each other.

You have given us a family that always has each other's backs as we try to live in a growing love relationship with you in a world that is often hard. We have learned to accept and love each other for who we are instead of telling you how to change each other into who we think you should make us to be. I know now that that isn't your love. We've often had to call on you for forgiveness and love as we make our journey together.

Romans 12:2: "And be not conformed to this world; but be ye transformed by the renewing of your mind, that ye may prove what is that good, and acceptable, and perfect will of God."

Romans 8:28: "And we know that all things work together for good to them that love God, to them who are the called according to his purpose. For whom he did foreknow he also did predestinate to be conformed to the image of his Son, that he might be the firstborn among many brethren."

You still create and give each human a free will to choose to be your child or not, but even as you create them, you already know who is going to choose you and who is not going to choose you. You are directing their life story to become like you, their Father. You created them to be in your image, which is loving and good. These two things are not incompatible with you.

Genesis 1:27: "So God created man in his own image, in the image of God created he him; male and female created he them."

I was teaching a first-grade Sunday school class in Florida when the superintendent brought Barry to me and said that Barry had recently got saved and wanted to learn to teach Sunday school, so he was putting him with me to learn. Barry sat on the little chairs with the first-graders while I taught, and he looked at me with his big brown eyes. I noticed his shiny black hair, black mustache, muscular body, and I thought he was really cute. I thought he must be so spiritual as he seemed to hang on every word I was teaching the children. He told me later that he was waiting for me to bend down to talk to the children so that he could see down the front of my dress. He liked the shape of me. I can't explain why Barry and I were drawn together, because we do seem a bit mismatched. Thankfully, your love never stopped working in Barry and I, no matter how stupid we sometimes acted.

The love and memories and lessons my dad taught me never left me though. My father was a good father in so many ways, and the love my human father gave me was one of the main pointers for me toward finding a relationship with you, the best father anyone can have. Even though my father developed some hard feelings toward me when I became an adult, this doesn't take away from what he gave me as a child and a teenager. The humans who raise us and the humans we are raised with become a part of who we are. Only you can fix this foundation when it has some serious flaws, or build on the good parts of the foundation to help us find a way to build our lives on Jesus, the true rock and foundation for our lives. One of the most wonderful things about heaven will be you unblocking the love flow for us completely. There will never be a relationship there that will have any blocks to a loving, growing eternal relationship, because we will be with you, we will be with ultimate love. Emotional loneliness and pain will be gone when we are all with you, our Father, in our eternal home, doing eternal life together.

Matthew 7:24-27: "Therefore whosoever heareth these sayings of mine, and doeth them, I will liken him unto a wise man, which built his house upon a rock; and the rain descended and the floods came, and the winds blew, and beat upon that house; and it fell not; for it was founded upon a rock. And everyone that heareth these sayings of mine, and doeth them not, shall be likened unto a foolish man, which built his house upon the sand; and the rain descended, and the floods came, and the winds blew, and beat upon that house; and it fell; and great was the fall of it."

My dad taught me how to influence children by interacting with them heart to heart, under your guidance. He taught me that a good way to do this is through stories and play and lots of fun, interactive attention. He made learning fun for me. He made wanting to know you fun for me. I wanted to become just like my daddy as a child and when I grew up, so happy to be serving you with my whole heart each day. You gave my dad the gift of evangelism. Whenever he talked with people, a lot of them would choose to become your children and follow you. My dad loved being a pastor for you, and I know you knew that this would be the career he would love the most when you called him into it. He always had time for me and the time he gave me was always fun. I always wanted to lead children to want to connect to your heart the way my dad did this for me when I was a child.

There are many reasons why I love working with children. Children naturally put love and friendship as their top priority. Children put having fun as their second priority. Children are so open to learn and be creative, since they haven't yet formed an opinion about much yet and they don't know the standard answers. They are funny and fun. Children so naturally place their trust in those who love and care for them. Childhood is such a special, open time to find you. They are so ready to believe in their heart's true hero. It has always made me happy inside to work with children and I am glad that you gave me this privilege.

Matthew 18:2–3: "And Jesus called a little child unto him, and set him in the midst of them. And said, 'Verily I say unto you, except ye be converted, and become as little children, ye shall not enter into the kingdom of heaven.'"

Dear God,

My dad first told me about how I could become your child when I was four years old. I asked my dad how he knew all this was true. He said I could read about it in your book, the Bible, and I told him I couldn't read yet. He said that I could just trust him that he had read your Bible and that is what it said. I said that I believed what he said and I received you as my Father without much understanding at all, but that is all it took to become yours. I came to you with very little understanding and I would have a lot of growing to do, but you entered me at that early age and I became forever yours and you became forever mine. This is partly how I know the children can truly become yours even when they are children. They don't have to wait until they are older, even if they truly come to you with very little understanding.

Later, when my brother was five and I was fifteen, I told him about you and he received you. I wasn't sure if he got it yet because later that same day he asked me to get him some ice cream. When I told him to wait until after supper he said that he needed it now because God was in his heart and God was hungry. As he grew, I saw that he was truly yours and had become yours without much understanding at all. I guess our understanding about you grows as our relationship with you grows, but it is so simple to become truly yours through repentance and faith.

I remember this when I am working with children. I never force them to receive you because that would never work. You have made it a free choice, and they need to respond to your heart calling to their heart, but I often tell them that, if they want to pray to you with me to receive you they can do this.

I remember as soon as I learned to read, I began reading the King James Bible because my dad told me that I could learn more about you in the Bible. There was this one verse that said to go in your closet every day and pray to you.

> Matthew 6:6: "But thou, when thou prayest, enter into thy closet, and when thou hast shut thy door, pray to thy Father which is in secret; and thy Father which seeth in secret shall reward thee openly."

My bedroom closet did not have a light so I decided to pray in the hall closet because it had a light in it that I could turn on. I had to hang on the shelves to be able to shut the door, but I was a kid so that was no problem. Sometimes I brought potato chips in with me, because you had not mentioned anything about not snacking as someone prayed. One time I had got myself all situated in the closet and I was just ready to pray when the house phone rang. All we had were landline phones back then. The phone was on a table right outside the closet, so I jumped out to answer it for my mom. Instead of saying hello, I said, "Dear Jesus," because I had just about been ready to pray to you. When I realized what I had done, I dropped the phone and ran and got my mom to tell her someone was on the phone line for her. After she got done talking to the lady, she came and talked to me. She said the lady had asked if Jesus often called us on the phone since we were a preacher's family. She was laughing. I told her about the verse and the closet. She explained that the word "closet" in the Bible just meant a room. I was relieved to just be able to go into my bedroom after this conversation and shut the door and pray without hanging onto the closet shelves anymore.

I guess it doesn't really matter how often we, your children, really don't understand things about you as long as we are trying our best to love, obey, grow with, and listen to you.

Then I remember when I reached middle age. Confronting middle age sometimes seems like reaching into a time bomb and either finding the right wire to cut in order to relieve us of disabling emotional negativity, or cutting the wrong wire and finding it all blowing up in our face. I wanted to confront the emotional negativity I had found myself in and let you reach into me to give me the fruits of your Spirit and a better life.

> Galatians 5:22–23: "But the fruit of the Spirit is love, joy, peace, longsuffering, gentleness, goodness, faith, meekness, temperance; against such there is no law."

I had decided not to give up my anger to you because I didn't want to become powerless. When I read verses in the Bible about giving my anger to you and never seeking revenge on anyone, and always forgiving everyone, I just blocked these in my mind by lying to myself and saying that you wouldn't apply these to me because you knew that I had been unfairly treated. You knew, as my mom's oldest child, that she had vented on me, trying to find a brief reprieve from the emotional and physical pain she found herself in. In spite of all the good that my mom had done me, I held a grudge against her for venting her anger on me to try to cope, and making me her willing slave, because I did care for her and wanted to help her. We always loved each other and had a relationship with each other, even though my emotional grudges kept my relationships bumpy, especially the ones with my mom and dad, because you can't really hide the brokenness inside, even if you never talk about it. Now I realize that you tell us to do things, because only by doing these things in the power of your Spirit can we be truly free and happy inside and live life the way you meant us to live it, changing evil into good internally with your love power.

I had decided not to give up my resentments to you because I didn't want to feel powerless, and by doing this I kept myself from your power. I felt so alone, like I had lost my connection with everyone, even you, and even myself. I felt so lost and afraid. It wasn't until Barry called me on the phone from his truck from a store parking lot that I finally decided to surrender to you. You knew I had to come to the end of myself to finally surrender and forgive everyone. Forgiveness doesn't mean that we try to deny that someone has caused us pain or that we can't find some good way to try to stop others from hurting us if it is possible. It just means we will never take any revenge and we will always pray for and seek the good for every other person that is involved in our lives, whether they have hurt us or not. I had been coping the same way my mother had tried to cope, only I had been venting my pain on Barry. I had been doing the exact same wrong thing, just trying to survive because I hadn't followed you to a better way.

I realized that I had destroyed all my relationships with my bad attitude, including the one with you, others, and myself. I thought about unfair treatment that I felt I had received in my life, recently from a Christian job, and also from people that I needed to be there for me. That summer Barry asked me to move out totally so he could have some time to think if he even wanted to continue our marriage or not. He started doing karaoke after work a lot with worldly friends to find fulfillment in being praised for his singing ability. He felt evil's pull to get his self-worth from trying to be famous through singing and receiving attention from the opposite gender. He didn't sleep with other women, but he went out singing with them and stopped caring how I felt. He felt just about as lost as I did. We missed you, ourselves, and each other a lot. We had been together over thirty years at this time, and after we were separated I would often feel I heard his voice calling my name at night.

I was sitting in the backyard on a swing when Barry called me on the phone and told me that he wanted to separate. I sat there and thought. I came to the end of myself. I decided to surrender my stubborn self-will to you. I felt like I was jumping out of an airplane without a parachute, and you caught me.

I found a place with you back in our personal garden, where I knew that even if I became homeless, living under a bridge, that I would be okay because I was safe in a place with the real and true God of the universe.

Barry and I had lived in a loving tug-of-war, but we had been having more than our usual trouble right before my dad died. My mom and I had some drama going on from my attitude, and of course my dad didn't like the way I was acting with my mother, so we never completely reunited before he died. I felt bad about this.

My father died suddenly of pancreatic cancer. He saw that I was trying to make amends before he died, but I'm not sure how much of it he actually believed. You used this time to bring my mom and I into the loving and forgiving relationship you had always desired for us to have. I don't know how you help with impossible things like this. You like jumping into people's messes and turning them totally around.

After my dad died, Ricky and I moved in with my mother for the summer so Barry could have his time. It is amazing how you are in every little coincidence. My mother and I reconciled in a beautiful way, with hearts of forgiveness and love. She helped me as I grieved the separation with my husband and maybe losing him forever. I helped her as she grieved the loss of my dad. He had always been so loving, kind, and good to her. It was very hard on her. I now thought about all the good my mother had done for me her whole life before I got married, and then helping me by taking care of Ryan while I worked after I got married, and all my bitterness just went away in a poof and if any bad feelings even tried to creep back after that, it was easy to block them because now I was letting your power work in my life instead of false power. I felt differently about you, others, and myself. I felt your love flow into my heart. I felt completely differently about my mother and our close friendship has never changed from that point on.

Ricky was about eleven at the time and you so protected him. He enjoyed going to my sister Serena's house because she lived near mom. He had fun playing with his cousins. My son Ryan and his wife also lived near there. Ryan told Ricky everything would be alright and mom and dad would work it out, he just had to be patient.

I know you don't like divorce because you don't like families to experience hurt. You love divorced people and you love children from divorced homes and you want to help them step through the issues caused by divorce with your love and guidance. I tried to follow your leading and not badmouth Barry to anyone, especially his sons. I just mostly tried to say and take responsibility for what I did wrong instead of what Barry did wrong. I said that my anger issues had brought a lot of this on, and I was trying to follow you more now. I texted Barry honest things kindly and tried to compliment him on things I felt were true. When I saw him, I tried to be loving, the way you would want me to. I wanted to do divorce your way, if it came to that, because I had started to realize that your way is always best.

My mom and I got so close and we resolved all our issues and became the best friends we had always wanted to be. Your timing, as always, was amazing, bringing my father home to you right when Barry and I were going through this so that my mom and I would be thrown together to help and care for each other right when we both needed it most. Also, how out of these terrible things we would come to the place of forgiveness and friendship from that point on. I guess timing and other types of coincidences are often not at all coincidental as you work out your amazing plans. You are also hiding from us in the miracles you bring to each of your children.

People can have almost any free will taken from them except the free will to love and be loved. Evil is like anti-God, anti-love, except without the power to negate, because nothing and no one has the power to extinguish you, the eternal, omnipotent, omniscient, just, and loving God.

Love is free will and I realized that I couldn't force Barry to stay with me—it had to be his choice. I showed him that I would no longer treat him with anger and control. I would try to treat him with respect and submission, but not submission to sin or contrary to your guidance. I can stand up to evil without practicing evil when I have your guidance.

The pull of love between a man and a woman is truly a mystery. When I was away from Barry, I missed him so much. I realized how much I had always needed him, and then his imperfections faded into the background as I thought about his good points and all he had meant to me and our children. I felt so rejected and I gave all my hurting emotions to you, and I felt you love me strongly through this hard time.

You showed me through this time that I had wanted to make Barry my Jesus or my emotional punching bag so that he could take my pain and the pain that life brings and fix everything for me and fix me. He had wanted to do the same with me. Please help me to never wrongfully hurt Barry again. Help me only and always to seek the good for others, even if they don't do the same for me, because showing your love is showing others how to join you in getting free from evil's traps. Give me the strength to love you, others, and myself always, no matter what life is bringing me and no matter who is bringing it. Help me to realize that Barry and I can never be Jesus to each other, because only Jesus has the power to be Jesus and that is part of the reason that you ask us to always put you first.

You taught me a lot at this time. It is amazing how a human's deepest distress can open their spirit and mind to see the truth of you, others, themselves, and your reasons for placing us in the world the way you placed us in it. I guess the knowledge of evil only makes us want your good that much more. I told Barry I was sorry and I told him what I appreciated about him and I tried to walk your transformed love walk when I was with him and when I wasn't. I tried to keep the relationship between Barry and our sons good. I tried to be more than fair and generous with money issues. I was preparing to go our separate ways when, surprisingly, you reunited Barry and I. Barry said that he never wanted to live without me again. He said that becoming a famous singer was no longer more important to him than being a husband and father. Ricky and I moved back into our home and my mother moved in permanently with my sister Serena. You took care of all of us. You used my greatest trial to give me a paradigm shift to become more intimate with you in the garden of your love. I may still lose my way sometimes, but I never forget that the garden is always there waiting for me, and that you will always help me find my way there if I just reach up for your hand.

Revelation 3:20: "Behold, I stand at the door, and knock; If any man hear my voice, and open the door, I will come in to him, and will sup with him, and he with me."

Dear God,

After Barry and I began living together again, I was walking back to my house from the store with Ricky. Ricky had walked home ahead and I was walking alone when I turned the corner. I felt the presence of my dad. I looked up at the clouds and I saw the blue sky and the white puffy clouds and I seemed to see my dad's invisible spirit spread out above me. I have never seen him this joyful on earth. This joy probably would have made him explode if it came to him on earth. There seemed to be silver spirals of joy emanating from him. I guess that is what happens when we finally get to really be completely with you.

My dad seemed to talk into my thoughts and said, "I'm glad you are finally loving your mother," and then he was gone. I guess he finally believed me.

I have thought about this a lot. It didn't seem like I dreamed or imagined it because I was fully awake and nothing like this has ever happened to me before or since. I'm not sure. Also, I was thinking about why would you let my dad nag at me from heaven. Then I was thinking that my dad wasn't nagging at me but he was trying to communicate to me that everything is all about you, it is all about love because you are the essence of love.

When your Bible has talked about believers appearing from the dead to interact a while on this physical earth, they seem to be able to shape-shift into how they looked while alive, and they seem to understand about the time and place people are experiencing on earth, as well as having a happy perspective of memories. People seem to know who each other are, even though they may have not known each other on earth. I know my dad has not received his new body yet and he didn't shape-shift into anything I could see, but I was able to be aware of his invisible presence and hear his words so clearly in my thoughts that it almost seemed that he spoke them aloud.

Matthew 17:3: "And, behold, there appeared unto them Moses and Elijah talking with him."

First Samuel 28:15: "And Samuel said to Saul, 'Why hast thou disquieted me, to bring me up?' And Saul answered, 'I am sore distressed; for the Philistines make war against me, and God is departed from me, and answereth me no more, neither by prophets, nor by dreams; therefore I have called thee, that thou mayest make known unto me what I shall do.'"

Your love made me real and the closer I get to you the more real you become to me. My sin blocks our communication even though you never disown me. I need you to be close so much.

Matter just transfers matter over and over throughout the ages. The only things on this earth that are not matter are the spirits that you placed in humans. You actually mixed your DNA with ours and became a God-man so that you could die as a perfect human to save us all. You went through all the stages of life as a human, a baby, a toddler, a child, a teenager, and an adult, and never gave in to the pull of evil because you are holy and without evil.

It is almost like this earth is a giant soccer game, with you and the devil as the coaches for each team. All your human children who died are the fans, watching and cheering as goals are made for good, and booing when goals are made for evil. They know they are on and cheering for the winning team because they know that when the game is over good will triumph as God's fire consumes all evil from the universe.

Hebrews 12:1: "Wherefore seeing we also are compassed about with so great a cloud of witnesses, let us lay aside every weight, and the sin which doth so easily beset us, and let us run with patience the race that is set before us."

Psalm 116:15: "Precious in the sight of the Lord is the death of his saints."

Hebrews 11:4: "By faith Abel offered unto God a more excellent sacrifice than Cain by which he obtained witness that he was righteous, God testifying of his gifts; and by it he being dead yet speaketh."

Second Corinthians 5:8: "We are confident, I say, and willing rather to be absent from the body, and to be present with the Lord."

Hebrews 12:29: "For our God is a consuming fire."

Dear God,

My dad was on fire for you until nearing the end of his life and then he started to be pulled into not seeing you as clearly, and that is the only time in all of his life that I saw him unhappy. You were drawing him back into closeness with you when he died. Then when I saw him in the clouds, I saw the joy in him that was greater than his happiest times on earth, and I knew that he was finally as close to you as he could get and he would never be drawn away again.

Dear Christie,

Don't stop seeing me in every beat of your heart. Don't stop seeing me in every helpful and good thought. Don't stop seeing me in the face of each newborn child. Don't stop seeing me in the beauty and life support system of the earth. Don't stop seeing me in the love and peace that comes to you internally when you trust and obey me. I don't like evil any more than you do and that is why I am fighting it. I had a time to call the earth into existence and I will have a time to call it out when I make all things new. I had a time for you to enter this earth and I will have a time to draw you out. You will retain the knowledge of good and evil that you learned here, which is the wish people had when they opened the door to evil. I granted this wish to humans and my children will learn more of why I hate evil but love them through this experience. Angels and believers will retain enough of this knowledge they have learned about evil that when it is finally gone from my universe they will never want to open this door again.

When this earth gets you down just remember that someday I will hug you and say, "Christie is finally home with us."

Dear God,

Then I will say that I will live forever in love and happiness in my daddy's home. Your love made me forever real. I am alive in your love. I was not real until you adopted me as your daughter. Now I can never be not real again. You are my Abba Father, God, and I am your daughter, and Jesus is my brother, and the Holy Spirit is my best friend. All the angels and human believers are my brothers and sisters. Our family will live together in joy.

Hebrews 11:6: "But without faith it is impossible to please him; for he that cometh to God must believe that he is, and that he is a rewarder of them that diligently seek him."

James 1:13: "Let no man say when he is tempted, I am tempted of God; for God cannot be tempted with evil, neither tempteth he any man."

Revelation 21:3–5: "And I heard a great voice out of heaven saying, 'Behold, the tabernacle of God is with men, and he will dwell with them, and they shall be his people, and God himself shall be with them, and be their God And God shall wipe away all tears from their eyes; and there shall be no more death, neither sorrow, nor crying, neither shall there be any more pain; for the former things are passed away.' And he that sat upon the throne said, 'Behold, I make all things new.' And he said unto me, 'Write, for these words are true and faithful.'"

Dear God,
I went to sleep and had a beautiful dream.

Dear Christie,
What was it?

Dear God,
I dreamed that my body died and suddenly I was running in a field of flowers. I was a little girl again, about four years old. My golden curls were bouncing as I ran with all my might. I was in a pretty dress and all I could think of was that my daddy was at the end of the field. As I was running, I was experiencing a total emotional, spiritual, and physical healing, and there was Jesus at the end of the field and he scooped me up into his arms and he hugged me and kissed my cheek and I hugged him with all my might. I felt the presence of you, God, the Holy Spirit, and Jesus all hugging me, and suddenly everything in the universe was right and would always be right. I looked around me and there were many little children, boys and girls of every human race, and Jesus was scooping them up as well since you can be personally there for each of us at the same time. Then Jesus put me down and my body quickly changed into a young adult, super-immortal woman. I looked to the side field and I saw my whole earthly life almost like a mirage and all the evil I had participated in was burned up in your fire and everything I had done from a loving heart toward you turned into a beautiful

crown. This was the only gift I had to give to you, the gift of my love. The other children also turned into young adults and I saw that they were seeing their lives the same way. Jesus took my hand and he took their hands and he led me and them into heaven where a huge celebration was going on and I knew that every day is better than Christmas here. I sensed an understanding of the beginning mystery of each person, like I did for humans I had loved on earth, only to a much greater degree. My parents and grandparents hugged me and I knew it was them even though they no longer looked old. And now we had changed into all being dear brothers and sisters. All the pull and drama of evil was totally gone. I never want any evil ever again, it is a destroyer of love and joy. Any grudges faded into complete forgiveness that brought understanding that caused even deeper love. All the angels and people became warm, fun, and loving friends. Then Jesus said, "Enter into the joy of the Lord." Things like joy, laughter, humor, friendship, love, peace, knowledge, fun, pleasure, purpose, creativity, belonging, and everything else you planted in me in my time on earth began to develop in ways I could have never imagined as soon as you enveloped me in your loving arms.

Chapter Four

Hell versus Heaven

JESUS IS OUR NORTH STAR

> Jesus is and has always been any human's North Star, always pointing the way to enter his family and have eternal life.
> His clues are often mysterious and our journey often includes strife.
> He forever mixed his deity with humanity to make it possible for us to have a God connection.
> He got the first immortal human body at his resurrection.
> He went through the complete human metamorphosis to show us how to do everything God's way.
> He loves like no one else can and he waits with joy for every believer to come home some glad day.
> After the Messiah came, people just needed to come to God in repentance and faith, going through the provided open door away from evil.

DAYDREAM OF HELL

Here is the story of two men who never received Jesus while they lived on the earth, and so they died without hope.
They did it their way, and that way in the end became a hanging rope.
Listen to their story and be wise:

Human Number One:
Every beautiful part of my life flashes before my eyes.
I see my mother, father, sister, brother, wife, children, and grandchildren with loving looks for me, and me for them.
The darkness is closing in and I feel a punishing, burning sensation, which makes me glad my consuming is coming quickly, as everything and everyone slips away and my heart cries.
God, I thank you for the life you gave me, even though it never became eternal, even though my acknowledgment of you, thankfulness to you, and yearning for you comes too late as I end.
Now that I know I will never have you as a Father and friend, I miss you, God.
God, I really loved riding that motorcycle with the wind in my hair.
God, I will say goodbye now as I fade away and disappear into ashes as I feel your justice rod.
God, I really loved making love to my wife without a care.
God, I'm sorry I wanted my own way and certain sins more than I wanted to find the clues you left to connect to you and follow you.
Thank you for sex, love, pizza, motorcycles, family, music, and life.
As I say my goodbye, I give my thanks and respect to you as the true God I never knew.
Since I didn't let you take my punishment by becoming your child through repentance and faith, I am glad to burn away now and be gone from all strife.

Human Number Two:
That other man just disappeared into nothingness and all I can do is stare.
I am a different man from him and I will gnash my teeth in anger, because life has been so unfair.

Even though I have to admit now that God is real and he is supreme, and God may have wanted all spirits to join him, I wanted to live my way, and of what he wants I really don't care.

God can't be all good because my life on earth was bad, and now in my afterlife I feel like I am being boiled until I am medium-rare.

I hope I go fast like that other man did.

Life had some pleasures, but mostly life stinks, and of life I will be glad to be rid.

I see some dark demon angel shadows and I see those aliens didn't fare any better than us humans did.

Everyone is suffering, and some suffer more than others, I welcome nothingness and soon from all pain I will be rid.

I would live my life the same way again, because I took care of me, lived my life on my own terms, and did everything my own way.

No matter who was trying to influence me, I'm glad I chose freedom instead of being bound to a twisted dictator's religious rules during the time I saw the light of day.

As I go and my last sparks fade away, all I can think of is: What was the point?

Burn in hell a long time, suckers, I'm leaving this joint.

HERE ARE TWO FALLEN ANGEL SPIRITS IN HELL

Fallen Angel Demon One:

I followed my true master here, and now look around at all the human souls we won, burning here with us.

Satan, though we suffer, we have won because you showed me how to be my own god and fight the control of God.

All the fallen angels and humans are now burning with you, Lucifer, since we gave you our trust.

We don't want to serve a God who causes any spirit who doesn't choose a connection with him to be burned away while being punished with a rod.

Influencing humans to greater degrees of sin was so exhilarating. Disconnection represents freedom to me.

I willingly take my punishment, and the fact I wanted my own way is not worth debating.

My memories of being with God are nothing but unwanted dreams because I no longer have eyes for the beauty of my creator to see.

Fallen Angel Demon Two:
I should never have left my true Creator.
I tried to help people be enlightened, good, and flow into the knowledge of the universe.
I saw that evil can never be good no matter what lies came from Satan, the great debater.
Only God is good and there is only one God and freedom comes from him and not from being sinfully diverse.
God, thank you for not making me eternal so that I do not have to suffer forever with regret.
I pray that your mercy would burn me away quickly so that I can be gone.
I disconnected from your love, and I never had anyone to pay that debt.
When I left you, I lost my heart's one true song.

GOD'S THOUGHTS WHILE DELIVERING FALLEN ANGELS AND UNBELIEVING PEOPLE TO HELL

If I did not have hell then I would turn into the devil and the universe would turn into hell and there would be no hope for anyone.
I have to punish sin, and now I have judged and it is time to punish, but I sorrow as I drop fallen angels and unbelieving humans into hell.
I wanted them to receive my love and be my children and share immortality when their spirit was linked to mine.
Instead of my truth, they embraced whatever lies were out there to sell.
After you have paid for however far you went into evil, my mercy will let you burn away.
You never became real in my love so your free-will choices have led you to be as if you had never been.
I grieve for the love we lost, dear fallen angels and unbelieving humans, but now all evil is contained and will be burned away and gone, and it is a bright new day.

Ezekiel 18:31–32: "'Cast away from you all your transgressions, whereby ye have transgressed; and make you a new heart and a new spirit; for why will ye die, O house of Israel? For I have no pleasure in the death of him that dieth,' saith the Lord God; 'Wherefore turn yourselves, and live ye.'"

Matthew 5:44-45: "But I say unto you, love your enemies, bless them that curse you, do good to them that hate you, and pray for them which despitefully use you, and persecute you; that ye may be the children of your Father which is in heaven; for he maketh his sun to rise on the evil and on the good, and sendeth rain on the just and on the unjust."

Psalm 37:20: "But the wicked shall perish, and the enemies of the Lord shall be as the fat of lambs; they shall consume; into smoke shall they consume away."

Matthew 8:12: "But the children of the kingdom shall be cast out into outer darkness; there shall be weeping and gnashing of teeth."

Philippians 2:11: "And that every tongue should confess that Jesus Christ is Lord, to the glory of God the Father."

Romans 9:22-24: "What if God, willing to shew his wrath, and to make his power known endured with much longsuffering the vessels of wrath fitted to destruction; and that he might make known the riches of his glory on the vessels of mercy, which he had afore prepared unto glory. Even us, whom he hath called, not of the Jews only, but also of the Gentiles."

Dear God,
I would like to talk about hell.

Dear Christie,
You almost seemed obsessed with this subject, but you are welcome to try to understand as best you can.

Dear God,
I am going to give a guess about what I think you are saying about heaven and hell. It was probably hard for you to make people and angels with free will because you knew right away which humans would never choose to turn to you, and your heart of love was sad to lose them. Your heart of justice was sad that they didn't let you help them overcome evil with good inwardly and outwardly on the earth. You hated the evil that people didn't let you help them fight against to the extent that they stepped into evil with their thoughts, actions, and words. You knew who the angels were who would choose to turn from you and your heart of love was sad to lose them. The destinies of all angel and human soul-spirits lie in how they choose to react to who you are with the free will you gave them. You had to endure the evil they decided to not let you take care of for them, because only in giving people and angels free will to choose or not choose you could you make beings to share real love with you. People can ask why you ever created spirit beings who you knew would reject you, but in creating them with a free will,

you didn't create them to reject you, even though you knew they would. You wanted all the angels and Adam and Eve to choose to stay linked with you. You wanted each human born to choose to link to you. I guess it is hard living out of time in the past, present, and future, yet trying to explain yourself to beings you created to live in time for now.

I am going to give you my guess as to what hell is all about. You are in ultimate control and you are good. You are in the process of completely eradicating evil. You are letting it into your universe for a time, but only for a time. You allowed evil to come in partly so sentient beings could learn about it experientially. Evil provided the ultimate evil choice of living unlinked to you. This is the only sin that causes an angel or human to enter hell. That is the choice of fallen angels to unlink from your Spirit and the choice of humans to never allow your Spirit to link to them by coming to you in repentance and faith with as little or much information as they have about the real you. This choice alone caused angels and people to never become real through surrender to the one we were created to be joined with. Our link to your Spirit links us to Jesus and you. While evil is allowed to remain here, you fight it with all your children and for us.

Matthew 12:31: "Wherefore I say unto you, all manner of sin and blasphemy shall be forgiven unto men; but the blasphemy against the Holy Ghost shall not be forgiven unto men."

Romans 8:14–16: "For as many as are led by the Spirit of God, they are the sons of God. For ye have not received the spirit of bondage again to fear; but ye have received the Spirit of adoption, whereby we cry, 'Abba, Father.' The Spirit itself beareth witness with our spirit, that we are the children of God."

Romans 8:9: "But ye are not in the flesh, but in the Spirit, if so be that the Spirit of God dwell in you. Now if any man have not the Spirit of Christ, he is none of his."

John 14:20: "At that day ye shall know that I am in my Father, and ye in me, and I in you."

Sometimes you let us feel the effects of evil as it runs its course, and sometimes you protect us from these effects. You knew about the idea and destructiveness of evil even before the first angel and first person let it come in. You have always loved angels and people, but hated evil and what evil does to them as they are pulled by it and hurt by it.

You knew that once evil was let into your universe, that you would be the only one capable of overcoming and extinguishing it forever with your love, power, mercy, and justice. You are the only one with the power and wisdom to overcome evil with good, and if you were not using your sacrificial love for your sentient spirits to do this, there would be no hope in the universe. You let us share in your work as your power flows through us to accomplish your purposes. Though your power is not limited to what you have flowing through your people children, this is your preferred method to get the gospel out and fight evil on the earth for now, I guess partly to keep everything in the realm of faith for now. The experiential knowledge of evil that people gained on earth will always help them understand why your good is so much better than evil. I think your angel children will have seen enough of how horrible and destructive evil is by helping you help your people children fight it, that none of them will ever want to let evil in again either. Maybe that was part of the reason that you allowed the door to evil to be opened in the first place, because how else would your sentient children really understand that you are truth, justice, righteousness, goodness, and love, if we didn't have any real experiential knowledge about why staying true to following your wise will about keeping evil out of your universe is so very important?

You alone are the Savior of the universe. You wanted real love with the sentient beings that you created and the only way to have that with them was to let them choose a connection with you over having freedom to do evil forever. Human and fallen angel philosophers said that you made people with immortal souls, but your Bible never says that anyone is immortal except you. Your Bible says that you only promise eternal life to people who let you link your Spirit to their spirit when they become your children through repentance to you and faith in you. Your Bible says the angels that never left you have not chosen to disconnect their spirit from your Spirit, and they also have eternal life by their connection to you, the one and only immortal being in the universe that is willing to share his immortality only with his children.

First Timothy 6:16: "Who only hath immortality, dwelling in the light which no man can approach unto; whom no man hath seen, nor can see; to whom be honour and power everlasting. Amen."

Luke 20:34–36: "And Jesus answering said unto them, 'The children of this world marry, and are given in marriage; but they which shall be accounted worthy to obtain that world, and the resurrection from the dead, neither marry, nor are given in marriage; neither can they die anymore; for they are equal unto the angels and are the children of God, being the children of the resurrection.'"

Dear God,

I guess at your rapture is when people start receiving their immortal bodies like the one Jesus has now. Once we have these, we will no longer need sex because there will be no more babies entering the world through us, and we all will have an emotional closeness of love with you and each other that transcends whatever pleasure and intimacy even earthly sex could produce. After the antichrist has his turn to rule seven years as the devil's man, and Jesus rules bodily on the earth for 1,000 years following the genetic line of the Jewish King David, then you will destroy the earth and the sky heaven with fire and make a new heaven and earth. You will make a new earth and sky heaven. You will judge fallen angels and unbelieving people and they will suffer in hell for however long and however painful your just punishment dictates for them until they burn away and are gone forever. Your believing humans and angels will live with you forever. Whatever work, play, adventures, learning, or anything else we are involved in will be free from evil's curse. It all really sounds too wonderful to be true, but all your Bible prophecies have come true so I know all this will come true as well, though my mind can't even really fathom anything so wonderful as being that close with you forever.

 I guess if you didn't punish evil then you would no longer be good. And if you turned evil, there would no longer be any hope to free the universe from the terminal destruction of evil's infection. Hell is necessary to burn evil, and any sentient being who chooses evil over you, away. The angels never got a second chance at redemption like people do. I guess since you made them as adults in heaven with you, they started off with more knowledge than humans. They knew enough to know they would eventually be punished and extinguished if they left you. Probably about one-third of them decided to go their own way anyway and they became demon fallen angels. You seem to have created each angel individually and they have no genetic link to each other. You seem to have created each angel as a soul-and-spirit sentient being, with a body completely different in substance than that of a human body. Angels seem to have a spirit body that you designed them with to project from their soul and spirit, and they can shape-shift into other forms at will. The ability of fallen angels to shape-shift into the human dimension or into the human mind seems to partly be controlled by what doors the humans they are involved with open for them. The spirit of the fallen angels is dead to you. They can enter many of the dimensions in your universe, staying under your boundaries, this would include the dimension of the material and of the soul. Fallen angel demons have to deal with the free will of humans and the boundaries of you, God, to keep working their power plays against you, God. They do not have a body like humans do or a genetic link like humans have. The infection of sin that each human is born with seems to be passed to us through our human father. Your redemption in the Messiah becoming a God-man, with a human mother but without a human father, and offering himself as a perfect human sacrifice for any people who wanted to receive this, was made possible by the genetic link that humans share through their bodies and that Jesus shares with us. Jesus wasn't born a sinner like every other human is, but he still could have chosen to sin like Adam and Eve did, and I'm so glad he didn't.

Romans 5:17: "For if by one man's offence death reigned by one; much more they which receive abundance of grace and of the gift of righteousness shall reign in life by one, Jesus Christ."

People were given less power and knowledge than the angels had when you made them. Fallen and unfallen angels will always have more knowledge and abilities than humans have while we are on this earth, but in a human's final metamorphic state in heaven we will have more power, wisdom, and abilities than we have now. However humans end up, all your angel and human children will all be completely submitting our wills to you as we grow with you and each other in love and freedom. People did not start out living with you like the angels did. People are born to live on a different planet than where you are, in a world created by you for them that you allowed fallen angels to interact with as they try to set up their own power structure apart from you. Even fallen angels have to stay within the boundaries that you give them if they want to stay out of a holding cell until the final judgment, and be free to interact, so they are stuck knowing you are overcoming their evil with good but trying to have as much power and evil fun as they can until they face their judgment and eventual extinction. They get evil pleasure out of trying to keep people from becoming your children and then if they do become your children, they try to keep them from growing close to you, because they don't want you to have any friends, especially when they see the love you share with your friends and which they have lost. They have to deal with the free will of humans and try to get them to submit to their powers in any tricky format they put out there. They don't want people to become your children and submit to you. They have become confused about what is good and evil, and they confuse people about what is good and what is evil.

Jude 1:6: "And the angels which kept not their first estate, but left their own habitation, he hath reserved in everlasting chains under darkness unto the judgment of the great day."

Matthew 12:43: "When the unclean spirit is gone out of a man, he walketh through dry places, seeking rest, and findeth none."

Unfallen angels stayed with you as your willing servants. The fallen angels had no power in this world until Adam and Eve sinned. At this point the devil was able to take over the kingdom of the world, but your kingdom is universal and you are in the process of taking the kingdom of earth back from the devil. When Adam and Eve chose to disconnect their spirits from yours, you offered them redemption, and they took it. Their bodies became slated for death, but it didn't happen instantly. Before Jesus died, unbelievers went to the soul sleep side of Hades or Sheol, and believers went to the paradise side of Hades or Sheol, where they were happy souls, aware and able to commune with God and do a lot of things, even though they were not yet in heaven.

Here is something I think your Scriptures are saying, if I am getting it right. After Jesus died, unbelievers continued to stay and go to Hades in soul sleep. They were unaware. They will remain there until the judgment and from there they will go to hell and burn away.

Hades is a type of prison where unsaved souls stay until they face the final judgment. These verses below seem to say that the preincarnate Christ encouraged people, through Noah, to come to him, but since they didn't, they are now in the prison of Hades. However, those who were spiritually baptized into Christ's family were not put in prison and will not die because they came to Christ through repentance and faith, even though they didn't completely understand that Jesus was the Messiah, part of the one true God that they followed. The sacrifices they offered before Jesus died were a symbol of what the Messiah would do, and the water baptism we do post-Jesus' death is a symbol of what the Messiah did for us.

First Peter 3:18–22: "For Christ also hath once suffered for sins, the just for the unjust, that he might bring us to God, being put to death in the flesh, but quickened by the Spirit; by which also he went and preached unto the spirits in prison; (They are in prison now. They weren't in prison when he was preaching to them through Noah.) which sometime were disobedient, when once the long-suffering of God waited in the days of Noah, while the ark was a-preparing, wherein few, that is, wight souls were saved by water. The like figure whereunto even baptism doth also now save us (not the putting away of the filth of the flesh, but the answer of a good conscience toward God) by the resurrection of Jesus Christ; who is gone into heaven, and is on the right hand of God; angels and authorities and powers being made subject unto him."

After Jesus died, he brought the souls of believers from the paradise side of Hades or Sheol to the paradise of heaven where all the souls of believers who die after this point go.

Ephesians 4:8–10: "Wherefore he saith, 'When he ascended up on high, he led captivity captive, and gave gifts unto men. Now that he ascended, what is it but that he also descended first into the lower parts of the earth? He that descended is the same also that ascended up far above all heavens, that he might fill all things.'"

Only Jesus has the immortal human body right now. At the rapture all believers whose bodies have died will be given an immortal body similar to the one that Jesus has now, and believers from then on will receive these at the point of their physical death. People could have lived forever on earth if they hadn't sinned, fellowshipping with Jesus with their alive spirit, soul, and body, as Jesus came into their material existence each evening. As soon as they let sin in, their spirit connection to God died, the earth they lived in was cursed with evil, their body would eventually decay and die, their spirit-soul would go to a holding place until the judgment and then it would die in the second death in hell, and Satan became the ruler of the earth. Every human will go through a bodily death, but their spirit-soul becomes eternally alive and escapes the second death of hell if they become God's child. The only way to fellowship with God on this earth now is in our consciousness, where out spirt and soul dwell, through prayer, Bible reading, listening to fellow believers, and faith, except for the few people who got to or will encounter Jesus as he bodily comes and leaves the earth in moments of time. The word "live" can have different meanings in your Bible. Sometimes you seem to use it to mean a believer whose body has died and their soul and spirit is alive with you. "Life" and "death" and "sleep" and "live" can get confusing sometimes the way you use them in the Bible because you view life and death and time so differently than we do. I don't think our physical death is very important to you compared with out spiritual death. You will probably cry and grieve for each angel or human soul/spirit that is lost to you as you drop them into hell's destruction.

Sleep often seems to refer to bodily death. It sounds so wild, if I am getting this right, when you say at a certain moment in time, starting with your rapture, you will give every human believer who has already died an immortal body, then you will suck up from the earth every believer to go immediately to heaven and they will quickly receive an immortal body at this time, and then every believer who dies after this time will immediately receive their immortal body right away instead of being a happy floating soul-spirit waiting to have an immortal body. I'm sure we can project bodily images with our soul/spirit, but it is not the same as having a real body. Then you will let the devil rule the world through the antichrist for seven years, Then you will have Jesus rule the world bodily for 1,000 years while the devil is in a holding place and some believers that have gone through the first death and have their new immortal bodies will get to be Jesus's assistants as he reigns for that thousand years. Then you will let the devil out of his holding place and you will have a final fight with the devil, after which you will destroy the earth and sky with fire and make a new sky-space heaven and earth that will be without evil.

At this point you will have your great white throne judgment and cast all the unbelieving people and fallen angel spirits into hell, where they will be punished and burned completely away and be gone almost as though they had never been. It will be eternal punishment for them, because they will never come back from it. It will not be like the metamorphosis that precedes this. How long and painful that eternity is for each one depends on the just punishment you hand down at your great white throne judgment. You will decide on the punishment for each person, and believers will be able to have their input as you decide on the punishment for the fallen angels.

You told us right after sin entered the world that Jesus, our Messiah, would come to fight the devil for all humans as the God-human. The devil hurts Jesus in this fight to the point of hurting his heel. Jesus will crush and destroy the devil's head until he is totally gone. Jesus is destroying the evil power in the kingdom of people bit by bit, as he was born with a genetic link to all humans, but yet remains fully God. He paid the price for the sin of every human who wanted to receive that gift when he offered his body as a perfect human sacrifice in death. You, God, are the head of the Trinity, so Jesus has always been a son to you in willing subordination, but he became your first complete immortal human son that went through the complete human metamorphosis when he received his immortal body at his resurrection. He will reign as earth's true king in his human body, starting with his millennial reign and going on forever after that.

Genesis 3:15: "And I will put enmity between thee and the woman, and between thy seed and her seed; it shall bruise thy head, and thou shalt bruise his heel."

Romans 1:3–4: "Concerning his Son Jesus Christ our Lord, which was made of the seed of David according to the flesh; and declared to be the Son of God with power, according to the spirit of holiness, by the resurrection from the dead."

Revelation 12:3–5: "And there appeared another wonder in heaven; and behold a great red dragon, having seven heads and ten horns, and seven crowns upon his heads. And his tail drew the third part of the stars of heaven, and did cast them to the earth; and the dragon stood before the woman which was ready to be delivered, for to devour her child as it was born. And she brought forth a man child, who was to rule all nations with a rod of iron; and her child was caught up unto God, and to his throne."

Matthew 4:8–11: "Again, the devil taketh him up into an exceeding high mountain, and sheweth him all the kingdoms of the world, and the glory of them; and saith unto him, 'All these things will I give thee, if thou wilt fall down and worship me.' Then saith Jesus unto him, 'Get thee hence, Satan; for it is written, "Thou shalt worship the Lord thy God, and him only shalt thou serve."' Then the devil leaveth him, and behold, angels came and ministered unto him."

First Corinthians 15:19–26: "If in this life only we have hope in Christ we are of all men most miserable. But now is Christ risen from the dead, and become the firstfruits of them that slept. For since by man came death, by man came also the resurrection of the dead. For as in Adam all die, even so in Christ shall all be made alive. But every man in his own order; Christ the firstfruits; afterward they that are Christ's at his coming. Then cometh the end, when he shall have delivered up the kingdom to God, even the Father; when he shall have put down all rule and all authority and power. For he must reign, till he hath put all enemies under his feet. The last enemy that shall be destroyed is death."

First Corinthians 15:42–55: "So also is the resurrection of the dead. It is sown in corruption; it is raised in incorruption; it is sown in dishonour; it is raised in glory; it is sown in weakness; it is raised in power; it is sown a natural body; it is raised a spiritual body. There is a natural body, and there is a spiritual body. And so it is written, 'The first man Adam was made a living soul; the last Adam was made a quickening spirit.' Howbeit that was not first which is spiritual, but that which is natural; and afterward that which is spiritual. The first man is of the earth, earthy; the second man is the Lord from heaven. As is the earthy, such are they also that are earthy; and as is the heavenly, such are they also that are heavenly. And as we have borne the image of the earthy, we shall also bear the image of the heavenly. Now this I say, brethren, that flesh and blood cannot inherit the kingdom of God; neither doth corruption inherit incorruption. Behold, I shew you a mystery; We shall not all sleep, but we shall all be changed. In a moment, in the twinkling of an eye, at the last trump; for the trumpet shall sound, and the dead shall be raised incorruptible, and we shall be changed. For this corruptible must put on incorruption, and this mortal shall have put on immortality, then shall be brought to pass the saying that is written, 'Death is swallowed up in victory. O death, where is thy sting? O grave, where is thy victory?'"

First Corinthians 6:3: "Know ye not that we shall judge angels? How much more things that pertain to this life?"

Daniel 7:22–26: "Until the Ancient of days came, and judgment was given to the saints of the Most High; and the time came that the saints possessed the kingdom. Thus he said, 'The fourth beast shall be the fourth kingdom upon earth, which shall be diverse from all kingdoms, and shall devour the whole earth, and shall tread it down and break it in pieces And the ten horns out of this kingdom are ten kings that shall arise; and another shall rise after them; and he shall be diverse from the first, and he shall subdue these kings. And he shall speak great words against the Most High, and shall wear out the saints of the Most High, and think to change times and laws; and they shall be given into his hand until a time and times and the dividing of time. But the judgment shall sit, and they shall take away his dominion, to consume and to destroy it unto the end."

Luke 12:46–48: "The lord of that servant will come in a day when he looketh not for him, and at an hour when he is not aware, and will cut him in sunder, and will appoint him his portion with the unbelievers. And that servant, which knew his lord's will, and prepared not himself, neither did according to his will, shall be beaten with many stripes. But he that knew not, and did commit things worthy of stripes, shall be beaten with few stripes. For unto whomsoever much is given, of him shall be much required; and to whom men have committed much, of him they will ask the more. I come to send fire on the earth; and what will I, if it be already kindled?"

Revelation 20:4—21:5: "And I saw thrones, and they sat upon them, and judgment was given unto them; and I saw the souls of them that were beheaded for the witness of Jesus, and for the word of God, and which had not worshipped the beast (anti-Christ empowered by the devil), neither his image, neither had received his mark upon their foreheads, or in their hands; and they lived and reigned with Christ a thousand years. But the rest of the dead lived not again (accessing the earth as well as heaven) until the thousand years were finished. This is the first resurrection. Blessed and holy is he that hath part in the first resurrection; on such the second death hath no power, but they shall be priests of God and of Christ, and shall reign with him a thousand years. And when the thousand years are expired, Satan shall be loosed out of his prison, and shall go out to deceive the nations which are in the four quarters of the earth, God and Magog, to gather them together to battle; the number of whom is as the sand of the sea. And they went up on the breadth of the earth, and compassed the camp of the saints about, and the beloved city; and fire came down from God out of heaven and devoured them. And the devil that deceived them was cast into the lake of fire and brimstone, where the beast and the false prophet are, and shall be tormented day and night for ever and ever. And I saw a great white throne, and him that sat on it, from whose face the earth and the heaven fled away; and there was found no place for them, and I saw the dead, small and great, stand before God; and the books were opened; and another book was opened, which is the book of life; and the dead were judged out of those things which were written in the books, according to their works. And the sea gave up the dead which were in it; and death and hell (hades) delivered up the dead which were in them; and they were judged every man according to their works. And death and hell (hades) were cast into the lake of fire. This is the second death. And whosoever was not found written in the book of life was cast into the lake of fire. And I saw a new heaven and a new earth; for the first heaven and the first earth were passed away; and there was no more sea. And I, John, saw the holy city, new Jerusalem, coming down from God out of heaven, prepared as a bride adorned for her husband, and I heard a great voice out of heaven saying, 'Behold, the tabernacle of God is with men, and he will dwell with them, and they shall be his people, and God himself shall be with them, and be their God. And God shall wipe away all tears from their eyes; and there shall be no more death, neither sorrow, nor crying, neither shall there be any more pain; for the former things are passed away.' And he that sat upon the throne said, 'Behold, I make all things new,' and he said unto me, 'Write; for these words are true and faithful.'"

Dear God,
These verses seem to indicate that the angels are learning more about your mercy, justice, and grace as they fulfill your purposes in helping you minister to your human children. They are also learning about why you don't want evil in your universe and what your connection to humans cost and costs you as you allow the fight to continue for your predetermined time before you shut it down. Maybe that is why you also made human sentient beings when you already had angel sentient beings.

First Peter 1:12: "Unto whom it was revealed, that not unto themselves, but unto us they did minister the things, which are now reported unto you by them that have preached the gospel unto you with the Holy Ghost sent down from heaven; which things the angels desire to look into."

Matthew 25:41: "Then shall he say also unto them on the left hand, 'Depart from me, ye cursed, into everlasting fire, prepared for the devil and his angels.'"

Dear God,
I think this shows that you long for each human to come to you and that you did not decide who would come to you and who would not, but each human decides. Each human is born lost to you until they choose to join your forever family.

Second Peter 3:9: "The Lord is not slack concerning his promise, as some men count slackness; but is longsuffering to usward, not willing that any should perish, but that all should come to repentance.

Mark 9:48: "Where their worm dieth not, and the fire is not quenched."

Since worms represent decay, I think this verse that says the worm dieth not means that they will continue to decay until they are gone. The fire is not quenched means they will burn until they are gone, and the decaying and burning of the second death process in hell will not be stopped until they are eternally gone.

Matthew 25:46: "And these shall go away into everlasting punishment; but the righteous into life eternal.

For humans, the only sin that will gain them entrance into hell will be not listening to the Holy Spirit's call for them to link to you in repentance and faith. They will not face judgment for their sins if they listen to the Holy Spirit's call to them to unite with you.

Mark 3:28–29: "Verily I say unto you, All sins shall be forgiven unto the sons of men, and blasphemies wherewith soever they shall blaspheme: But he that shall blaspheme against the Holy Ghost hath never forgiveness, but is in danger of eternal damnation:"

Ephesians 2:8–9: "For by grace are ye saved through faith; and that not of yourselves; it is the gift of God; Not of works, lest any man should boast."

Not forgiving someone doesn't send someone to hell and stop them from being your child, but it keeps you from communicating and working with them on this earth in showing us the right way to deal with the influence of sin.

Matthew 6:14–15: "For if ye forgive men their trespasses, your heavenly Father will also forgive you; But if ye forgive not men their trespasses, neither will your Father forgive your trespasses."

Ephesians 4:30: "And grieve not the holy Spirit of God, whereby ye are sealed unto the day of redemption."

Ephesians 4:15: "But speaking the truth in love, may grow up into him in all things, which is the head, even Christ."

Dear God,

When I love a friend or relative and I long for the love of this friend or relative to be returned to me, my sorrow is so great that if I do not call on your power to forgive that person for not loving me back and give them to you with well wishes for their life, I think nothing could swallow me alive like the pain of rejection. I am so sorry that any of your sentient beings would ever reject your love because no one would ever be able to love them the way that you can. No one could rescue, redeem, and transform them the way your love can. No one could synergistically mix with them in intimacy the way you can link with them in love. I am so sorry that you ever feel the pain of rejection that you would never feel if your love was not so deep.

Isaiah 53:3: "He is despised and rejected of men; a man of sorrows, and acquainted with grief; and we his as it were our faces from him; he was despised, and we esteemed him not."

You do not let humans on the earth truly see beyond death. I guess this is part of your plan to put the connection of us to you into the realm of faith. Your Bible seems to say different things about the human afterlife. This could be because of the Bible going in and out and jumbling up the human timeline depending on what you were letting your prophets see of the past, present, and future events from the point of human time that they prophesied in. I guess you did not need to create time until you created humans, so it seems like you often give us what we need to know jumbled up in the human timeline that we live in.

I know you are a personal God and you form a personal love link with each of your children through Jesus. Even all true believers are going to have varying perspectives about what you mean about things in your Bible depending on denominations, family backgrounds, timelines, skill sets, spiritual giftedness, spiritual maturity, personal perspectives, personal strengths, personalities, how much they are surrendered, tasks you plan for them to fulfill, and other factors that involve them. You are like a diamond with many facets, and many humans could be seeing you many different ways and all be right as long as they are seeing some aspect of your truth. I'm not talking about false gods that are the opposite of the way you revealed yourself in the Bible. I'm talking about us, your human children on earth, seeing the real you in varying perspectives.

I know we are not supposed to get angry if we do discuss any of these things with other humans, but talking about hell can easily get everyone angry. Sometimes it is better just to agree that the Bible is true and the only way to you is faith in the real you and in the provision you provided to forgive our sins in your Messiah, than it is to try to reach agreement on every topic with each other. It is impossible in this world to know the complete truth but we can all get the simple main truth about becoming your children by coming to you in repentance and faith.

Our differing strengths and weaknesses are all part of each of us being a different part of your ministering body, with you as the head. Only in you is our diversity unified, harmonized, and fulfilled. We never stop being the individuals you made us to be, but in connecting to you, we find an amazing love connection to all of your children through you that will blossom into mind-blowing proportions in heaven.

Romans 12:4-6: "For as we have many members in one body, and all members have not the same office; so we, being many, are one body in Christ, and every one members one of another. Having then gifts differing according to the grace that is given to us, whether prophecy, let us prophesy according to the proportion of faith."

Dear God,

From my limited perspective in researching the Bible, I would like to discuss more of the subject of hell with you. I know things will clear up a lot at the end of earth time, but I would really like to think it through a little bit. I know that what I think or don't think about this has nothing to do with becoming your child or not becoming your child. I know you are truth and what I think doesn't change the truth of who you are and why you do what you do. I know you only have a good purpose in everything you do. I can fellowship with any true believer, no matter how many secondary things we disagree on. I don't want to argue with anyone, and I'm not sure how right I am getting things, but please just help me think it through.

Second Corinthians 4:18: "While we look not at the things which are seen, but at the things which are not seen; for the things which are seen are temporal; but the things which are not seen are eternal."

Dear God,

Every human will deal with evil as they live out this earthly life. Sometimes it is hard for us to understand how you are letting evil play out during our earth time. We all see one of the consequences of evil when we see human death. One day someone is here and interacting, and the next day they are just gone and we can't see where they go. Sin always hurts everyone it touches. Your differing laws with differing human consequences were given to people since the beginning of earth time as protective boundaries and to show them that it is impossible for humans to overcome evil ourselves. Evil is so devastating that only you are good enough to overcome it, and humans can only become eventually completely free from it in heaven. Only you have the wisdom and power to extinguish evil from your universe. You are letting this war play out within your boundaries for as much time as it takes to have each human child come to you who you already know will choose to come to you. When that very last human is born, earth time will end.

Sin is a destructive trap that can pass through generations. However, you are brilliant enough to use the evil that comes into a person's life plan or that a person is pulled toward to work out your plan in that person's life. Testing, consequences, and trials of evil in a person's life, whether that person is the innocent victim or the one doing evil, have the possibility to give the person more wisdom, insight, love, growth, faith, courage, and strength in you, or to pull a person away from the truth about you. The devil never knows which way things are going to go when he finds his openings to propagate evil in people's lives, but you do. Every human is born lost to you and your desire is for every human to let you find him or her. Satan's desire is to keep every human from connecting to you in any way. Believers never have to go through your final judgment, but you have to judge fallen angels and unbelievers very justly or you would turn evil yourself.

Luke 19:10: "For the Son of man is come to seek and to save that which was lost."

Job 34:10-15: "Therefore hearken unto me, ye men of understanding; far be it from God, that he should do wickedness; and from the Almighty, that he should commit iniquity. For the work of a man shall he render unto him, and cause every man to find according to his ways. Yea, surely God will not do wickedly, neither will the Almighty pervert judgment. Who hath given him a charge over the earth, or who hath despised the whole world? If he set his heart upon man if he gather unto himself his spirit and his breath; all flesh shall perish together, and man shall turn again unto dust."

Dear God,
There will be no more need for faith in heaven. We will no longer have to wrestle with what is true and what is false, what is fantasy and what is reality, what is evil and what is good, what is your voice in our thoughts and what is another voice, what is imagination and what is faith. We will no longer feel the pull of sin, and our intimacy with you, others, and ourselves will finally be what we have always longed for on this earth. Glimmers of true love shown on this earth only give us a taste of what heaven will be like all the time for all of us.

Since, unlike angels, all humans have some kind of genetic connection to each other, I think you created people to all be connected to each other through a set of one first parents so that evil came to all through one, and so salvation could come to all through one if anyone chooses to receive this gift from you.

Romans 5:18: "Therefore as by the offense of one judgment came upon all men to condemnation; even so by the righteousness of one the free gift came upon all men unto justification of life."

First John 4:17–19: "Herein is our love made perfect, that we may have boldness in the day of judgment; because as he is, so are we in this world. There is no fear in love; but perfect love casteth out fear; because fear hath torment. He that feareth is not made perfect in love. We love him because he first loved us."

Dear Christie,
You seem afraid to get to your point.

Dear God,
I think the more truth we discover about you, the more we feel your perfect love and the less false fear we feel. The more we love you, others, and ourselves with your love, the more we feel your true love flowing through us and back to you again, and our faith in you increases. When we feel your love and guidance, we can go through anything and remain happy inside ourselves, living in your friendship as you bring us through anything good or bad with your guidance, wisdom, strength, love, power, and joy. Everything on this earth is temporary for me except my connection to you.

Dear Christie,
I love you with the most powerful love of all. Please try to get to your point.
Romans 8:35–39: "Who shall separate us from the love of Christ? Shall tribulation, or distress, or persecution, or famine, or nakedness, or peril, or sword? As it is written, 'For thy sake we are killed all the day long; we are accounted as sheep for the slaughter.' Nay, in all these things we are more than conquerors through him that loved us. For I am persuaded that neither death, nor life, nor angels, nor principalities nor powers, nor things present, nor things to come nor height nor depth nor any other creature, shall be able to separate us from the love of God, which is in Christ Jesus our Lord."

Dear God,
I know you know everything so I know that you knew what it was going to cost you to make sentient spirit beings with a free will so they could choose whether or not to have a love relationship with you. Adam and Eve could have lived forever, perfectly, on a perfect earth, with intimate fellowship with you if they hadn't chosen sin, but this doesn't mean that you created them immortal. I don't see any verses that say that you created humans and angels immortal yet I have heard it said that you are never going to let the people and angels eventually burn away and die in the second death of hell. I don't think you would have created them immortal since you knew

some angels were going to leave you and some humans were not going to choose you. You offer eternal life to humans who choose to become your children through repentance and faith. It seems like you give eternal life to the angels who never left you. I think all the other angels and humans will be burned away and gone in hell. They will be thrown in hell after the final judgment and begin their punishment in time and severity in hell until they are burned away and gone. I'm not sure if I am getting all this completely right or not.

John 8:44: "Ye are of your father the devil, and the lusts of your father ye will do. He was a murderer from the beginning, and abode not in the truth, because there is no truth in him. When he speaketh a lie, he speaketh of his own; for he is a liar, and the father of it."

Revelation 20:10: "And the devil that deceived them was cast into the lake of fire and brimstone, where the beast and the false prophet are, and shall be tormented day and night for ever and ever."

Dear God,

I know Jesus talked about hell a lot when he was on the earth. I'm not sure I know what he was saying, but I am guessing. I know he died to keep people from having to go there. I think Jesus was telling people that if they were not going to receive his salvation that they should at least keep as much of God's moral laws as they could so that the severity of the punishment that they receive in hell will be a lot less. I think Jesus was saying that those who have the chance to know more of the truth about God because of the time and place they live in, and still choose to reject him, will be punished more severely than those who only learn a little about the true God because of the time and place they live in. However, every human has a chance to choose to connect to the true God no matter what time or place they live in because your Spirit calls to each human spirit to come to you.

Romans 1:17-25: "For therein is the righteousness of God revealed from faith to faith; as it is written, 'The just shall live by faith.' For the wrath of God is revealed from heaven against all ungodliness and unrighteousness of men, who hold the truth in unrighteousness; because that which may be known of God is manifest in them; for God hath shewed it unto them. For the invisible things of him from the creation of the world are clearly seen, being understood by the things that are made, even his eternal power and Godhead; so that they are without excuse; because of that, when they knew God, they glorified him not as God, neither were they thankful; but became vain in their imaginations, and their foolish heart was darkened. Professing themselves to be wise, they became fools, and changed the glory of the uncorruptible God into an image made like to corruptible man, and to birds, and fourfooted beasts, and creeping things. Wherefore God also gave them up to uncleanness through the lusts of their own hearts, to dishonor their own bodies between themselves; who changed the truth of God into a lie, and worshipped and served the creature more than the Creator, who is blessed for ever. Amen."

It seems like fallen angels that cross your boundaries go to an abyss somewhere to wait for the judgment. The devil will be put in this pit or abyss for 1,000 years when Jesus reigns on earth for the millennium.

I'm thinking, correctly or incorrectly, that when people are born, their body begins the death process, but they don't die right away. Eventually their body dies and their spirit and soul leave their body. This is the first death. When fallen angels and unbelievers enter hell, they do not die right away, after they have served the sentence of their judgment of time and severity in hell, they will be burned away in the second death. Believers will never experience the second death. Eternal fire and eternal punishment may mean that there are no more changes once someone is in hell. Your Bible never says "eternal death," it says "second death" or "destruction" or "perish." They are slated to be burned and gone forever, not connected to their Creator. Believing people who are part of the rapture will not have to go through the first death, which the Bible often calls sleep.

First Corinthians 15:51–57: "Behold, I shew you a mystery; we shall not all sleep, but we shall all be changed, in a moment, in the twinkling of an eye, at the last trump; for the trumpet shall sound, and the dead shall be raised incorruptible, and we shall be changed. For this corruptible must put on incorruption, and this mortal must put on immortality. So when this corruptible shall have put on incorruption, and this mortal shall have put on immortality, then shall be brought to pass the saying that is written, 'Death is swallowed up in victory. O death, where is thy sting? O grave, where is thy victory?' The sting of death is sin; and the strength of sin is the law. But thanks be to God, which giveth us the victory through our Lord Jesus Christ."

Psalm 37:20: "But the wicked shall perish, and the enemies of the Lord shall be as the fat of lambs; they shall consume; into smoke shall they consume away."

Matthew 8:29: "And, behold, they cried out, saying, 'What have we to do with thee, Jesus, thou Son of God? Art thou come hither to torment us before the time?'"

Matthew 8:12: "But the children of the kingdom shall be cast out into outer darkness; there shall be weeping and gnashing of teeth."

Philippians 2:11: "And that every tongue should confess that Jesus Christ is Lord, to the glory of God the Father."

Romans 9:22-24: "What if God, willing to shew his wrath, and to make his power known, endured with much longsuffering the vessels of wrath fitted to destruction; and that he might make known the riches of his glory on the vessels of mercy, which he had afore prepared unto glory. Even us, whom he hath called, not of the Jews only, but also of the Gentiles."

Luke 12:48: "But he that knew not, and did commit things worthy of stripes, shall be beaten with few stripes. For unto whomsoever much is given, of him shall be much required; and to whom men have committed much, of him they will ask the more."

First Peter 1:12: "Unto whom it was revealed, that not unto themselves, but unto us they did minister the things, which are now reported unto you by them that have preached the gospel unto you with the Holy Ghost sent down from heaven; which things the angels desire to look into."

Luke 20:35-36: "But they which shall be accounted worthy to obtain that world, and the resurrection from the dead, neither marry, nor are given in marriage; neither can they die any more; for they are equal unto the angels; and are the children of God, being the children of the resurrection."

Obadiah 1:15-16: "The day of the Lord is near for all nations. As you have done, it will be done to you; your deeds will return upon your own head. Just as you drank on my holy hill, so all the nations will drink continually, they will drink and drink and be as if they had never been."

Isaiah 14:12-15: "How art thou fallen from heaven, O Lucifer, son of the morning! How art thou cut down to the ground, which didst weaken the nations! For thou hast said in thine heart, 'I will ascend into heaven, I will exalt my throne above the stars of God; I will sit also upon the mount of the congregation, in the sides of the north; I will ascend above the heights of the clouds; I will be like the Most High.' Yet thou shalt be brought down to hell, to the sides of the pit."

Revelation 12:7-9: "And there was war in heaven; Michael and his angels fought against the dragon; and the dragon fought and his angels. And prevailed not; neither was their place found any more in heaven. And the great dragon was cast out, that old serpent, called the Devil, and Satan, which deceiveth the whole world: he was cast out into the earth, and his angels were cast out with him."

Ezekiel 28:13-19: "Thou hast been in Eden the garden of God; every precious stone was thy covering, the sardius, topaz, and the diamond, the beryl, the onyx, and the jasper, the sapphire, the emerald, and the carbuncle, and gold; the workmanship of tabrets and of thy pipes was prepared in thee in the day that thou was created. Thou art the anointed cherub that covereth;

and I have set thee so; thou wast upon the holy mountain of God; thou hast walked up and down in the midst of the stones of fire. Thou wast perfect in thy ways from the day that thou was created, till iniquity was found in thee. By the multitude of thy merchandise they have filled the midst of thee with violence, and thou hast sinned; therefore I will cast thee as profane out of the mountain of God; and I will destroy thee, O covering cherub, from the midst of the stones of fire. Thine heart was lifted up because of thy beauty, thou hast corrupted thy wisdom by reason of thy brightness; I will cast thee to the ground, I will lay thee before kings, that they may behold thee. Thou hast defiled thy sanctuaries by the multitude of thine iniquities, by the iniquity of thy trafficked; therefore will I bring forth a fire from the midst of thee, it shall devour thee, and I will bring thee to ashes upon the earth in the sight of all them that behold thee. All they that know thee among the people shall be astonished at thee; thou shalt be a terror, and never shalt thou be any more."

Second Thessalonians 1:9: "Who shall be punished with everlasting destruction from the presence of the Lord, and from the glory of his power."

Matthew 25:30, 41, 46: "And cast ye the unprofitable servant into outer darkness; there shall be weeping and gnashing of teeth. . . . Then shall he say also unto them on the left hand, 'Depart from me, ye cursed, into everlasting fire, prepared for the devil and his angels.' . . . And these shall go away into everlasting punishment; but the righteous into life eternal."

Dear God,

Every statement Jesus said was true. Every story the writers of the Bible wrote was true. However, all the stories Jesus told the people to help them understand spiritual things are all fiction, with nonfiction meanings hidden inside, so I think this story about Abraham talking to the rich in Hades would be a parable like every other story Jesus told. Help us try to decipher the hidden meanings in the parable with your Holy Spirit's help. It is not always that easy. I think Jesus gave this parable about two people who went to the good and bad sides of Hades or Sheol to show us that all decisions are final after death and we can't cross back and forth. He used the name Abraham because people knew Abraham was saved by repentance and faith even before your Messiah died. He could have different reasons for choosing to use the name Lazarus for the poor beggar because this parable could have more than one message. He told the story that if the rich man was cast into his punishment in hell while he was still in Sheol instead of going into soul sleep until the judgment, and if people could talk back and forth from the good and bad sides of Hades or Sheol, this would probably be the conversation. The torment was jumping ahead to the torment that people will receive when the unbelieving side of Hades is cast into hell after the judgment. Almost certainly people couldn't talk back and forth and see each other from each side, but Jesus was saying what the conversation would be if they could. Also, the unbelieving side is in soul sleep until the judgment. Jesus is showing that no matter how a person's life is on earth, once that person is dead, there are no more chances at redemption and people on earth can only become God's children through repentance and faith.

Luke 16:19-26: "There was a certain rich man, which was clothed in purple and fine linen, and fared sumptuously every day; and there was a certain beggar named Lazarus, which was laid at his gate, full of sores, and desiring to be fed with the crumbs which fell from the rich man's table; moreover the dogs came and licked his sores. And it came to pass, that the beggar died, and was carried by the angels into Abraham's bosom; the rich man also died, and was buried; and in hell he lift up his eyes, being in torments, and seeth Abraham afar off, and Lazarus in his bosom. And he cried and said, 'Father Abraham, have mercy on me, and send Lazarus, that he may dip the tip of his finger in water, and cool my tongue; for I am tormented in this flame.' But Abraham said, 'Son, remember that thou in thy lifetime received thy good things, and likewise Lazarus evil things; but now he is comforted, and thou art tormented. And beside all this, between us and you there is a great gulf fixed; so that they which would pass from hence to you cannot; neither can they pass to us, that would come from thence.'"

Dear God,
I think these verses in Luke 10 show that unbelievers will not start their punishment until after the judgment.

Luke 10:14-16: "But it shall be more tolerable for Tyre and Sidon at the judgment, than for you. And thou, Capernaum, which art exalted to heaven, shalt be thrust down to hell. He that heareth you heareth me; and he that despiseth you despiseth me; and he that despiseth me despiseth him that sent me."

Dear God,
I think these verses in Ephesians show that Jesus took the good side of Hades to heaven after he died. Hades or Sheol seem to be located under the earth and heaven seems to be located somewhere with you, above the earth and the atmosphere or the sky heaven covering the earth.

Ephesians 4:8-10: "Wherefore he saith, 'When he ascended up on high, he led captivity captive, and gave gifts unto men. Now that he ascended, what is it but that he also descended first into the lower parts of the earth?

He that descended is the same also that ascended up far above all heavens, that he might fill all things.'"

Dear God,

It is hard to understand exactly what you are saying here. You seem to be saying that the unbelievers that Noah preached to, that died in the flood, are now in a type of prison and they are not in hell yet. You seem to be saying that Noah preached to them with the power of Jesus' Spirit when they were alive on the earth. You seem to be saying that you gave them time to turn to you, and that you were disappointed that only eight people allowed you to save them from the flood.

First Peter 3:18–20: "For Christ also hath once suffered for sins, the just for the unjust, that he might bring us to God, being put to death in the flesh, but quickened by the Spirit; by which also he went and preached unto the spirits in prison; Which sometime were disobedient when once the longsuffering of God waited in the days of Noah, while the ark was a preparing, wherein few, that is, eight souls were saved by water."

Ecclesiastes 3:18–21: "I said in mine heart concerning the estate of the sons of men, that God might manifest them, and that they might see that they themselves are beasts. For that which befalleth the sons of men befalleth beasts; even one thing befalleth them; as the one dieth, so dieth the other; yea, they have all one breath; so that a man hath no preeminence above a beast; for all is vanity. All go unto one place; all are of the dust, and all turn to dust again. Who knoweth the spirit of man that goeth upward, and the spirit of the beast that goeth downward to the earth?"

Dear God,

I think in these verses from Ecclesiastes 3, Solomon seems to be saying that animals and people both turn to dust when they die. However, the soul of an animal is gone forever while the soul of an unbelieving human goes into some kind of soul sleep while waiting for the final judgment. In these following verses in Ecclesiastes and Psalms, I think Solomon and David are also saying this same thing again, if I am getting it right.

Ecclesiastes 9:10: "Whatsoever thy hand findeth to do, do it with thy might; for there is no work, nor device, nor knowledge, nor wisdom in the grave, whither thou goest."

Psalm 6:5: "For in death there is no remembrance of thee; in the grave who shall give thee thanks?"

Psalm 88:12: "Shall thy wonders be known in the dark and thy righteousness in the land of forgetfulness?"

Psalm 115:17: "The dead praise not the lord, neither any that go down into silence."

Dear God,
I think these Bible writers are showing that believers have and always will have awareness after death in happy communication with you.

Hebrews 11:4: "By faith Abel offered unto God a more excellent sacrifice than Cain, by which he obtained witness that he was righteous, God testifying of his gifts; and by it he being dead yet speaketh."

Philippians 1:23–24: "For I am in a strait betwixt two having a desire to depart, and to be with Christ; which is far better. Nevertheless to abide in the flesh is more needful for you."

Second Corinthians 5:8: "We are confident, I say, and willing rather to be absent from the body, and to be present with the Lord."

Hebrews 12:1: "Wherefore seeing we also are compassed about with so great a cloud of witnesses, let us lay aside every weight, and the sin which doth so easily beset us, and let us run with patience the race that is set before us.

Mark 12:26–27: "And as touching the dead, that they rise; have ye not read in the book of Moses, how in the bush God spake unto him, saying, 'I am the God of Abraham, and the God of Isaac, and the God of Jacob?' He is not the God of the dead, but the God of the living; ye therefore do greatly err."

First Samuel 28:11–15: "Then said the worman, 'Whom shall I bring up unto thee?' And he said, 'Bring me up Samuel.' And when the woman saw Samuel, she cried with a loud voice; and the woman spake to Saul, saying, 'Why hast thou deceived me? For thou are Saul.' And the king said unto her, 'Be not afraid; for what sawest thou?' And the woman said unto Saul, 'I saw gods ascending out of the earth.' And he said unto her, 'What form is he of?' And she said, 'An old man cometh up; and he is covered with a mantle.' And Saul perceived that it was Samuel, and he stooped with his face to the ground, and bowed himself. And Samuel said to Saul, 'Why hast thou disquieted me, to bring me up?' And Saul answered, 'I am sore distressed; for the Philistines make war against me, and God is departed from me, and answereth me no more, neither by prophets, nor by dreams; therefore I have called thee, that thou mayest make known unto me what I shall do.'"

Dear God,
I think these verses also show that even if our sins cause our own early physical death, you never take our salvation away from us once we are your child. The punishing, sinful, consequential, or suicidal death of our body

does not kill our spirit link to you, even if we got to the point where we allowed our sin to block your Holy Spirit's communication to us in our earthly life. Nothing kills our spirit link to you once we are your child and you have removed hell from our afterlife. Those who die early from delving too far into sin from capital punishment or getting caught in traps or even from commiting suicide never stop being your children, and they still come to you at their death and never have to go to hell. Sometimes it is a blessing to think about this when we think of how weak we can all be at times.

Revelation 20:11–15: "And I saw a great white throne, and him that sat on it, from whose face the earth and the heaven fled away; and there was found no place for them. And I saw the dead, small and great, stand before God; and the books were opened; and another book was opened, which is the book of life; and the dead were judged out of those things which were written of those things which were written in the books, according to their works. And the sea gave up the dead which were in it; and death and hell delivered up the dead which were in them; and they were judged every man according to their works. And death and hell were cast into the lake of fire. This is the second death. And whosoever was not found written in the book of life was cast into the lake of fire."

First Corinthians 15:20–23: "But now is Christ risen from the dead, and become the firstfruits of them that slept. For since by man came death, by man came also the resurrection of the dead. For as in Adam all die, even so in Christ shall all be made alive. But every man in his own order; Christ the firstfruits; afterward they that are Christ's at his coming."

Luke 23:43: "And Jesus said unto him, 'Verily I say unto thee, today shalt thou be with me in paradise.'"

When sin entered the world and people died, their body did not die right away, but it would die eventually. Their soul did not die right away, but it would die eventually unless they let Jesus redeem it with their spirit. Their spirits died right away. They lost their connection to God. When a human comes to Jesus in repentance and faith, he gives them a new spirit. Their soul is connected to their spirit in such a way that it will follow their spirit into eternity. Their body will return to the earth, but someday they will be given a new body to clothe their soul and spirit.

Malachi 3:17—4:1: "'And they shall be mine,' saith the Lord of hosts, 'in that day when I make up my jewels; and I will spare them, as a man spareth his own son that serveth him. Then shall ye return, and discern between the righteous and the wicked, between him that serveth God and him that serveth him not. For, behold, the day cometh, that shall burn as an oven; and all the proud, yea, and all that do wickedly, shall be stubble; and the day that cometh shall burn them up,' saith the Lord of hosts, 'that it shall leave them neither root nor branch.'"

Dear God,
Jesus forever mixed his divinity with humanity to pay the price for all humans so the could have the chance to pursue good rather than evil by choosing you. You make the spirit of those humans who chose you synergistically come alive and they receive eventual immortality as part of your gift. Their bodies will see decay at the first death but their spirit, soul, conscience, mind, will, and emotions—in other words, their essence—will never see decay and never go into the second death in hell.
Mark 9:48: "Where their worm dieth not, and the fire is not quenched."

Dear God,
Humans never turn into angels, but we will share similarities to them in our final stage of life. We will no longer marry. We will no longer die.
Mark 9:47: "And if thine eye offend thee, pluck it out; it is better for thee to enter into the kingdom of God with one eye, than having two eyes to be cast into hell fire; where their worm dieth not, and the fire is not quenched."
Matthew 3:11-12: "I indeed baptize you with water unto repentance; but he that cometh after me is mightier than I, whose shoes I am not worthy to bear; he shall baptize you with the Holy Ghost, and with fire; whose fan is in his hand, and he will throughly purge his floor, and gather his wheat into the garner; but he will burn up the chaff with unquenchable fire."
Philippians 3:19-21: "Whose end is destruction, whose God is their belly, and whose glory is in their shame, who mind earthly things. For our conversation is in heaven; from whence also we look for the Saviour, the Lord Jesus Christ; who shall change our vile body, that it may be fashioned like unto his glorious body, according to the working whereby he is able even to subdue all things unto himself."
Matthew 26:39: "And he went a little further, and fell on his face, and prayed, saying, 'O my Father, if it be possible, let this cup pass from me; nevertheless not as I will, but as thou wilt.'"
Hebrews 12:2: "Looking unto Jesus the author and finisher of our faith; who for the joy that was set before him endured the cross, despising the shame, and is set down at the right hand of the throne of God."

Dear God,
Am I getting this right?

Dear Christie,

You will eventually find out for sure won't you? Don't let my justice keep you from seeing my love. Don't let my holiness keep you from seeing my mercy. Trust that I saved you from hell when there was no way for you to save yourself and I did this at the price of seeing my only son go through a lot of pain just so that I could have the joy of you becoming my child and sharing my home in heaven eternally. Jesus and the Holy Spirit and I did all this for you because we want you to be part of our family. I know you don't feel worthy but my transforming love is making you worthy, because you can't make yourself worthy to be my friend and I want your love and friendship for eternity. I was willing to do this and I did it and I am doing it.

Dear God,

Thank you! I love you. I'm so sorry for all my sins. I want to believe in you more. I want to follow you more. Thank you for loving me in a way no one else can love me, even myself. I wish everyone would know your love. I wish I would never hurt you by doing any evil, but I know I do hurt you like this. I'm sorry. Thank you for helping me love you better as I grow closer to you, because I really want to love and follow you better so you will know I love you.

Matthew 19:21: "Jesus said unto him, 'If thou wilt be perfect, go and sell that thou hast, and give to the poor, and thou shalt have treasure in heaven; and come and follow me.'"

Dear God,

I guess there is no way for any person to be sinless enough to be able to overcome evil on their own. That is why you sent us your Messiah. Thank you.

Revelation 21:7-8: "He that overcometh shall inherit all things; and I will be his God, and he shall be my son. But the fearful, and unbelieving, and the abominable, and murderers, and whoremongers, and sorcerers, and idolaters, and all liars, shall have their part in the lake which burneth with fire and brimstone; which is the second death."

Revelation 2:23: "And I will kill her children with death; and all the churches shall know that I am he which searcheth the reins and hearts; and I will give unto every one of you according to your works."

Dear God,

I'm guessing when the Bible says forever that it means until they are gone. Just like when your Bible talks about the slave that will serve his master forever, we know that it means until he dies.

Exodus 21:5-6: "And if the servant shall plainly say, 'I love my master, my wife, and my children; I will not go out free,' then his master shall bring him unto the judges; he shall also bring him to the door, or unto the door post; and his master shall bore his ear through with an awl; and he shall serve him forever."

Romans 3:20: "Therefore by the deeds of the law there shall no flesh be justified in his sight; for by the law is the knowledge of sin."

Psalm 119:105: "Thy word is a lamp unto my feet, and a light unto my path."

First John 2:16-17: "For all that is in the world, the lust of the flesh, and the lust of the eyes, and the pride of life, is not of the Father, but is of the world. And the world passeth away, and the lust thereof; but he that doeth the will of God abideth forever."

First John 5:7: "For there are three that bear record in heaven, the Father, the Word, and the Holy Ghost; and these three are one."

First John 5:12: "He that hath the Son hath life; and he that hath not the Son of God hath not life."

Matthew 5:22: "But I say unto you that whosoever is angry with his brother without a cause shall be in danger of the judgment; and whosoever shall say to his brother, *Raca*, shall be in danger of the council; but whosoever shall say, 'Thou fool,' shall be in danger of hell fire."

Dear God,
I think Jesus was saying here that it is better for us to give any sin that we want to keep to you instead of letting that sin keep us from coming to you in repentance and faith.

Matthew 5:29: "And if thy right eye offend thee, pluck it out, and cast it from thee; for it is profitable for thee that one of thy members should perish, and not that thy whole body should be cast into hell."

Romans 3:20-26: "Therefore by the deeds of the law there shall no flesh be justified in his sight; for by the law is the knowledge of sin. But now the righteousness of God without the law is manifested, being witnessed by the law and the prophets; even the righteousness of God which is by faith of Jesus Christ unto all and upon all them that believe; for there is no difference; for all have sinned, and come short of the glory of God; being justified freely by his grace through the redemption that is in Christ Jesus; whom God hath set forth to be a propitiation through faith in his blood, to declare his righteousness for the remission of sins that are past, through the forbearance of God. To declare, I say, at this time his righteousness that he might be just, and the justifier of him which believeth in Jesus."

Dear God,

The devil doesn't want anyone to be your friend. He seems to keep people from coming to you, or growing in you when they come to you, by getting people to believe lies about you. He often uses the evil that he helped bring into existence, and that you are extinguishing, to get people to not see your overcoming goodness. He confuses people about who is evil and what evil is. It becomes so hard for us to see through the delusions and lies of this world whenever we take our eyes off of you. The devil often uses partial truths to get us to believe his lies about you.

Isaiah 14:14: "I will ascend above the tops of the clouds; I will make myself like the Most High."

Dear Christie,

Learn who I really am. I've got this (Ps 90:2; 139:7; 1 John 3:20; 4:8; Jer 32:17; Isa 44:24; Job 34:12; Rev 1:8).

Second Corinthians 5:8: "We are confident, I say, and willing rather to be absent from the body, and to be present with the Lord."

First John 2:16–17: "For all that is in the world, the lust of the flesh, and the lust of the eyes, and the pride of life, is not of the Father, but is of the world. And the world passeth away, and the lust thereof; but he that doeth the will of God abideth forever."

Dear God,

Your heart of love wants to share your eternity with your human and angel friends. This will be a place where you are always the center and your love will flow to them, through them, back to you, and to each other. The dream became full of nightmares, but someday all the nightmares will be gone because you are powerful enough to do this. Thank you for making me, wanting me, and loving me. Deep in every person is a longing for the story of the hero to overcome evil with good. Jesus is the ultimate superhero. Thank you for making angels and believing humans part of your family and kingdom, your sons and daughters, your princes and princesses, and mostly, your forever friends. I may not understand why you set up the earth as you did or exactly what heaven and hell will be like and why you need to enact a specific plan to overcome evil with good, but I know enough about you personally to trust you with everything I don't know and can't figure out. Help me to stop going around in circles and grow more in my wisdom, love, and trust in you. I love you.

Psalm 23:4: "Yea, though I walk through the valley of the shadow of death I will fear no evil; for thou art with me; thy rod and thy staff they comfort me."

Hebrews 12:2: "Looking unto Jesus, the author and finisher of our faith; who for the joy that was set before him endured the cross, despising the shame, and is set down at the right hand of the throne of God."

Psalm 78:39: "For he remembered that they were but flesh; a wind that passeth away, and cometh not again."

Psalm 73:12–27: "Behold, these are the ungodly, who prosper in the world; they increase in riches. Verily I have cleansed my heart in vain, and washed my hands in innocency. For all the day long have I been plagued, and chastened every morning. If I say, I will speak thus; behold I should offend against the generation of thy children. When I thought to know this, it was too painful for me. Until I went into the sanctuary of God; then understood I their end. Surely thou didst set them in slippery places; thou castedst them down into destruction. How are they brought into desolation, as in a moment. They are utterly consumed with terrors, as a dream when one awaketh; so, O Lord, when thou awakest, thou shalt despise their image. Thus my heart was grieved, and I was pricked in my reins. So foolish was I, and ignorant; I was as a beast before thee. Nevertheless I am continually with thee; thou hast holden me by my right hand. Thou shalt guide me with thy counsel, and afterward receive me to glory. Whom have I in heaven but thee? And there is none upon earth that I desire beside thee. My flesh and my heart faileth; but God is the strength of my heart, and my portion for ever. For lo, they that are far from thee shall perish; thou hast destroyed all them that go a whoring from thee."

Dear Christie,
I am just, good, loving, kind, powerful, fair, immortal, generous, all-knowing, everywhere at once, and merciful.

Dear God,
Here is my take on this and I know that you always love me and keep me as your child no matter how many things I may get right or wrong about you as I journey on my relationship with you. All of us humans that are your children have misunderstandings about your words and your ways but you still use us in your battle and love and lead us in our relationship with you. There is nowhere in the Bible where it says that you ever created angels or humans to be immortal. There is nowhere that the Bible says anyone is immortal except you. That is why I think you did not create people and angels to be immortal, although that might have been an impossibility anyway because there may be some things about being God that cannot be replicated since there is only one God and you are it.

Your justice demanded death for humans for contaminating themselves with evil, but that was definitely combined with your mercy. Your mercy let their soul and spirit dwell in their body for a time so that they could choose you and learn things before their body died and their soul and spirit left their body. Your mercy allows their body not to live forever in evil's miseries and the death of the body becomes a blessing as evil's curse takes its toll on each human and their body turns back into the soil that you created the first human body from.

Dear Christie,
John 10:9-11: "I am the door; by me if any man enter in, he shall be saved, and shall go in and out, and find pasture. The thief cometh not, but for to steal, and to kill, and to destroy; I am come that they might have life, and that they might have it more abundantly. I am the good shepherd; the good shepherd giveth his life for the sheep."

Dear God,
My heart beats for you and my soul sings for you. When I don't understand and I am afraid, I reach for you and you always take my hand and help me through to the other side. I remember when I was sixteen and I began working summers in a nursing home to earn money for college. I was working from three to eleven p.m. It was a rude awakening for me. It started with me putting a man's body in a huge garbage bag to be taken away. I had listened to him having the death rattles all day and then he died, and since I was new, I got the job of putting his body in the bag to be ready for the people to come and take him away. He didn't seem to have any you or any family or money. This was a poor nursing home where unwanted people were placed to die. The nurses gave the people drugs at night to take away their pain and help them sleep.

One night, after we had fed and changed everyone and settled them in for the night, I was walking the dim hallway alone. I heard moanings and groanings coming from various rooms. I desperately cried out to you and said in my mind, "God if this is how humans end up, what is the point of human life?"

You answered me clearly in my mind and said, "This is not the end, it is the only the beginning."

I guess that it is the beginning of real life for believers and I guess that it is the beginning of the merciful end for unbelievers who never became real in your love.

Dear God,

Here is my daydream about how quick earth life is where we make our choices and learn about why you hate evil and about what you value and love, which is all of your children, and we learn to value and love you here by faith until we are really with you and no longer need faith.

My baby Ryan sat on my lap outside and reached for the clouds. He thought he could touch them. He grew and grew and became God's child and he became married to a sweet Christian woman and had two children, Tony and Tina.

I find myself sitting in my bedroom, remembering a special time in my life. The sun was shining brightly as my father and I walked up to my grandma's house when I was still a very young child. We walked to her bed, and her wrinkled hands clasped both my father's and my hands. She held our hands very tightly as she stared into our faces so intently with a wise and sad look I could not understand.

I remember my grandmother stared into my face; I was too young to fathom her age or the seriousness of her communication. I tried to concentrate, but my mind drifted to a butterfly I saw fluttering in the grass outside her window. I wished I was chasing it away from this solemn mood.

I tugged on my father's sleeve, and my grandmother's kind eyes penetrated deeply into mine. I realized at that moment that she was dying.

Now, I am a grown-up lady, and I shake my head clear and see the bright sunlight coming into my window as I sit on my bed. I better get going or I will be late for work.

I am startled by a knock on my bedroom door. As I listen to my own crackly voice answering, "Come in," I realize with a start that I forgot just how old I have become and that I don't work anymore.

A tall, handsome, thirty-something man comes into my bedroom with a little girl. Slowly, I realize that the man is my grown son, Ryan, and the child is my very own granddaughter, Tina.

Were those wrinkled hands reaching out to grasp the man's and the little girl's hands mine? How did they get so wrinkled? I grip Tina's hands tighter, hoping it will keep me from disappearing. Ryan runs to get Barry and Ricky.

My granddaughter, Tina, has soft skin and large, curious eyes. She does not yet know the pain that life can give. The seriousness of our meeting makes her fidgety. I can see her eyes drift to a butterfly outside my window, and I remember when I was at her place on the human timeline and my grandmother was at the place I am now on the human timeline.

I look deeply into her beautiful childlike face, feeling parts of me pass to her as our generations circle. She will soon be one of the few things left of me in the world. Our eyes meet in a sad and affectionate good-bye, as we both realize that I am dying.

As I drop Tina's hand, I see Ryan lead her into the other room and call for Barry and Ricky to come. They enter, and the picture of their dear faces grows dim. I feel the sweet presence of my God as I have never felt him before. As I fade away to an unknown world, I hope my Lord Jesus will gather me into his arms and comfort my fear in my transitioning metamorphosis.

Surely the one who has created the beauty, pleasure, and love in this world will have something even better in the perfect next world where evil's pull will be gone and where I can live in our home with the love of my life. A smile of hope comes to my face as I die and Jesus gathers me into his loving arms.

> Dear Christie,
> Can you stop talking about hell now?

> Dear God,
> Yes, thank you. When I am in complete internal turmoil and you clear up my confusion, it builds my faith and trust in you. When my internal is okay with you, the good or bad things that happen externally lose their emotional pull on me as I flow more into your eternal perspective and wisdom.
> Galations 5:22–23: "But the fruit of the Spirit is love, joy, peace, longsuffering, gentleness, goodness, faith, meekness, temperance; against such there is no law."

All of your creation and functionalities on this earth are pointers to you and who you are and what you are really all about. Thank you for making me real with your love.

Revelation 20:12, 21:1–6: "And I saw the dead, small and great, stand before God; and the books were opened; and another book was opened, which is the book of life; and the dead were judged out of those things which were written in the books, according to their works."

Chapter Five

Triangular Wisdom

Dear God,
So many of your Scriptures, at first glance as I am reading them, appear to be oxymorons or contradictions. I had a dear Christian friend that got so derailed by these that she got lost in what was truth and what wasn't truth to such an extent that she was afraid to have children because she was so confused about what truth to teach them. Satan can use these things to keep people from coming to you or to lead your human children into a floundering place where they are unable to move forward in their faith with you. I know that your intentions were for connection in reaching to adopt human friends into your family. That is why you made them in your image and linked them with you. We never become you, you are still you and we are still us, but you make us synergistic partners with you. You will always be the highest and no one will ever be like you or completely be able to understand you, so you wanted us to trust you as we forever grow in our understanding and faith in you.

Your Scriptures often seem to talk in opposites at first glance. I guess that is because these things are like the bottom corners of a triangle, and at the top point where they meet at is where your higher wisdom and thoughts dwell. You are the one and only God, the Trinity, Three Persons in One, which are You, God the Father; Jesus, the Son; and the Holy Spirit. You love each other totally and completely and you have your own identities while your identity is together. You offer your children a link to you and your love.

We are never you and you are never us. I think the main similarity between humans and angels is that you created us both with a spirit so that we could choose to be linked forever to your love. Satan is always attacking our identity because having our identity in you is the best thing there is and he hates this. Jesus provided that human link for humans born lost and dead to you in sin. If we receive the link that Jesus provided for us, we still go through the first death of our body, but we will never go through the second death of our soul and spirit. The only thing we have to do to become truly alive and your forever children is come to you in repentance and faith, which means that we will try to follow you as our guide and keep you first while we live out our days with as little or as much information as we have. Only then does your love make us real as we are born again, linked to your Spirit. This real life includes a thought connection from you to us and us to you. This real life includes an eventual eternal life with you, with a soul, spirit, and body that is free from all evil. If we are not linked to you, we never become real, and will eventually burn away in hell and be gone forever someday, along with the fallen angels.

First John 5:7-8, 12: "For there are three that bear record in heaven, the Father, the Word, and the Holy Ghost; and these three are one. . . . He that hath the Son hath life; and he that hath not the Son of God hath not life."

Isaiah 55:8-9: "'For my thoughts are not your thoughts, neither are your ways my ways,' saith the Lord."

I will try to guess at what you mean when some verses appear contradictory. The first verses are about forgiveness. Some of your verses seem to say that if we don't forgive other people for the wrongs they do to us, and if we don't give to you whatever revenge we would seek toward them, in order to do as you will, that you will not forgive us. Other verses seem to say that when we come to you in repentance and faith, you immediately make us your forever child, and nothing can ever break that link. The link will not be broken if we continue to sin, which we will do and fight against doing until our body dies. Your Holy Spirit will always work on our hearts to ask for your continual forgiveness for the sin we do as your children and your power to stop whatever sinning we are doing as your child.

I think your triangular wisdom means that once we come to you in repentance and faith, we are your forever children and nothing can break that link. We will not go to hell or stop being your child even if we don't forgive others the way you want us to. You forgive our sins completely, as far as us ever having to spend any time in hell, as soon as we become your children, even though we will sin again on this earth, and even though one of those sins may be falling into the trap of unforgiveness. When we forgive others, you show us your forgiveness on earth by helping us move spiritually forward. We could even try to stand up to try to get them not to hurt us anymore, as long as we do it under your good direction. If we forgive in your way, you will help us heal from the pain evil caused us and use us as lights to show others your amazing, loving power. We will block ourselves from hearing your voice in our thoughts and from having our identity grow in our shared friendship if we don't forgive. We will become trapped in such a way that we will tend to manifest the evil that was done to us to ourselves and others in differing ways, instead of being free from that particular root of evil that may have been an opening for evil spirits to influence our thoughts. Part of being your child means you never stop working on us to conform us more and more into your image, and that includes showing us why it is so important to forgive others. We learn that your preferred vengeance is transformational love. Until we actually seek no revenge, internally or externally, toward anyone that has ever done us wrong, we block your love that is flowing to us and out of us and back to you and back to us again. Once we are your child, we never stop being your child, and your forgiveness of our sins destines us for heaven and not hell, and this will never change. But our ability to hear from you and receive help from you depends on our responses to the evil that touches us.

We show to the one who wronged us your kindness, love, and forgiveness through well-wishing prayers and actions that you lead us to do. In doing this, we remember that you are all about love and redemption in the way that you overcome evil with good. We may or may not trust the person enough to continue a relationship with that person as you direct us, but we can always continue to pray your blessing for that person, whenever that person comes to mind. We can always continue to leave our heart's door open for renewed friendship, if that person ever truly becomes yours and begins to follow your ways. Only you are sinless, powerful, and wise enough to bring the final judgment on a human or fallen angel's sin at the final judgment.

Matthew 6:14–15: "For if ye forgive men their trespasses, your heavenly Father will also forgive you; but if ye forgive not men their trespasses, neither will your Father forgive your trespasses."

John 6:37–40: "All that the Father giveth me shall come to me; and him that cometh to me I will in no wise cast out. For I came down from heaven, not to do mine own will, but the will of him that sent me. And this is the Father's will which hath sent me, that of all which he hath given me I should lose nothing, but should raise it up again in the last day. And this is the will of him that sent me, that every one which seeth the Son, and believeth on him, may have everlasting life; and I will raise him up at the last day."

Matthew 22:36–40: "'Master, which is the great commandment in the law?' Jesus said unto him, 'Thou shalt love the Lord thy God with all thy heart, and with all thy soul, and with all thy mind. This is the first and great commandment. And the second is like unto it, Thou shalt love thy neighbour as thyself. On these two commandments hang all the law and the prophets.'"

I think the other concept that seems to be ambiguous is how we have a free choice to become your child or not, even though so many things about our lives are not free choices. Even though you knew who would become your child and you chose to adopt them, you never took away the free will choice from each human you created to become your child or not. We never had the choice to be born or not. We never had the choice where we would be born in earth time or the place we would be born on earth. We never had the choice of what family, race, and culture that we would be born into. We never had the choice of what strengths we would be born with. Yet you say letting you adopt us or not as your child is a free choice for us from the time we are old enough to be aware of you until our soul-spirit leaves our physical body at our first death. Yet you ask us to bring all that we are to you, become your child, and always put you first no matter where that path may lead. I guess we have to trust that you have the best intentions for our internal life, even if following you may cause us physical problems and sometimes even death in this life. All humans will die, and fear won't keep us from dying. We can be willing to take the risks that following you may bring us by remembering that you will always be with us through our earthly journey and our physical death. Then you will transition us to eternal life with you, where there will be no more death. You say surrendering to you in repentance and faith is the only way to become real, and that we can only become who you meant us to be when we are linked to you. People were becoming your children through repentance and faith before they even really understood what your Messiah was all about or that his name was Jesus. They just followed you in repentance and faith and began a conversation with you as they lived out their lives in friendship with you, always seeking to put you first.

People who die before they are consciously aware of your Spirit's pull to them, either because they are too young or disabled, never reject or blaspheme the link your Spirit holds out to them to become your children. Dying with this rejection still in place is the only sin that sends people to hell, so babies are born into sin, but they never commit the sin of rejecting your Spirit's call into their soul, so they enter your home at their bodily death. Everyone who dies when they are old enough to accept the link your Spirit holds out to each human as he calls into each human's heart to come to you in repentance and faith, admitting your supreme Lordship by doing this, becomes your forever child. Those who are old enough to hear your Spirit's call to their heart, but refuse it, never become real in your love and they are destined to burn away.

Isaiah 7:16: "For before the child shall know to refuse the evil, and choose the good, the land that thou abhorrest shall be forsaken of both her kings."

Ephesians 1:4-13: "According as he hath chosen us in him before the foundation of the world, that we should be holy and without blame before him in love; having predestinated us unto the adoption of children by Jesus Christ to himself, according to the good pleasure of his will. To the praise of the glory of his grace, wherein he hath made us accepted in the beloved. In whom we have redemption through his blood, the forgiveness of sins, according to the riches of his grace; herein he hath abounded toward us in all wisdom and prudence; having made known unto us the mystery of his will, according to his good pleasure which he hath purposed in himself; that in the dispensation of the fulness of times he might gather together in one all things in Christ, both which are in heaven, and which are on earth; even in him; in whom also we have obtained an inheritance, being predestinated according to the purpose of him who worketh all things after the counsel of his own will; that we should be to the praise of his glory, who first trusted in Christ. In whom ye also trusted, after that ye heard the word of truth, the gospel of your salvation; in whom also after that ye believed, ye were sealed with that Holy Spirit of promise."

Second Samuel 12:22-23: "And he said, 'While the child was yet alive, I fasted and wept; for I said, "Who can tell whether God will be gracious to me, that the child may live?" But now he is dead, wherefore should I fast? can I bring him back again? I shall go to him, but he shall not return to me.'"

Matthew 12:31: "Wherefore I say unto you, all manner of sin and blasphemy shall be forgiven unto men; but the blasphemy against the Holy Ghost shall not be forgiven unto men."

Revelation 3:20: "Behold, I stand at the door, and knock; if any man hear my voice, and open the door, I will come in to him, and will sup with him, and he with me."

Romans 10:10: "For with the heart man believeth unto righteousness; and with the mouth confession is made unto salvation."

Dear God,

I think another thing that is hard to understand is how you created each one of us individually, with seeds of self-development that you had in mind to bloom in us as a body, soul, and spirit, yet we need to link with you for this to completely happen. How do we separate you from us and yet not separate you from us?

I always tell the children in my class that you put certain emotional, physical, skill-related, personality, and learning styles, as well as intelligence and strengths in each human child at conception. After that child becomes your child, then you even put certain spiritual strengths in each one. I tell them to try everything that they may think may look like fun as they are growing up because they may discover that that thing is something you planted in them to do very well, and if they don't try it, they may never find all the amazing gifts that you planted in them. Some of them will discover that they are full of potential to be amazing singers, artists, actors, mathematicians, scientists, naturalists, athletes, comedians, musicians, writers, politicians, teachers, preachers, historians, businesspeople, linguists, mechanics, engineers, missionaries, builders, cleaners, parents, counselors, friends, social helpers, philosophers, healers, merchants, and any other skill form out there. You made us to be better together. You made us to be even better together when we are personally connected to you. You made us to need you and each other and ourselves in a love-flowing way under your directions.

We never become you and you never become us, but we are synergistically connected to you when we become your child so that your thoughts flow to us and our thoughts flow to you. We can't be as intimate with anyone else except you. We can't really be alive and joined to your universe without being connected to you, no matter what high substitutes the devil wants to offer people with his religious fallen angels offering a plethora of substitutes for the real thing. He gets as close as he can get, but he can never make us real, and evil in any form always becomes destructive. When we try to take your place in our own lives or in anyone else's life instead of continuously giving control back to you, even when our life journey seems beyond our comprehension or abilities to handle, we see you work everything out for your good because you make us good when we are joined to you. You can even use the evil on the earth and even use people that don't become your children on their life journey to accomplish your purposes. You even use people that are your children at whatever stage of spiritual development they are in to accomplish your good purposes in overcoming evil with good in their sentient life and in all sentient life that belongs to you.

You knew Pharaoh was never going to become your child and that he was always going to try to show that he was the greatest false god. He was influenced by the lies of evil spirits, just like so many before them have been. Evil spirits offer themselves as false gods throughout time in whatever ways they can trick people into accepting. They were behind the Greek and roman gods, idols, sorcerers, and other satanic connectors. They are behind psychics, spells, witches, warlocks, wiccans, illuminati, familiars, satanic books, secret societies, some governmental power leaders, astrologists, spiritisms, spirit guides, mediums, satanic games like tarot cards, crystal balls, and Ouija boards, and any false religion that veers from the truth of the Bible. Pharaoh felt like he was synergistically connected with Satan, sort of like the antichrist will feel one day, that he is the top earth power that should be worshiped and followed. I don't think it is smart to pick a fight with you, God.

Exodus 9:14–17: "For I will at this time send all my plagues upon thine heart, and upon thy servants, and upon thy people; that thou mayest know that there is none like me in all the earth. For now I will stretch out my hand; that I may smite thee and thy people with pestilence; and thou shalt be cut off from the earth. And in very deed for this cause have I raised thee up, for to shew in thee my power; and that my name may be declared throughout all the earth. As yet exaltest thou thyself against my people, that thou wilt not let them go?"

Since all the spirits connected to you have been made good by you, even though your earthly human spirits are not fully experientially good until their spirit-soul leaves their body, and your unfallen angels are good, this passage in 1 Samuel about you sending the evil spirit to Saul must mean that you gave the devil permission to invade the protection you have on your children for that time. When you do this and one of your children are close to you, they do not lose their inward peace from you. When you do this because one of your children has opened doors to fallen angels to allow them to enter, even though that human is your child, they totally lose their peace from you.

First Samuel 16:15–17: "And Saul's servants said unto him, 'Behold now, an evil spirit from God troubleth thee. Let our lord now command thy servants, which are before thee, to seek out a man, who is a cunning player on a harp and it shall come to pass, when the evil spirit from God is upon thee, that he shall play with his hand, and thou shalt be well.' And Saul said unto his servants, 'Provide me now a man that can play well, and bring him to me.'"

Dear God,

Just because you had us born in a certain time and a certain place with certain strengths and weaknesses planted within us doesn't mean you took away our free-will choice to listen to the voice of your Spirit and come to you in repentance and faith. Just because you live in all time and knew ahead of time what humans you created would come to you and which ones would not come to you doesn't mean that you took away the free choice that you gave each human in their earth time, or that you haven't called into the spirit of each human born to become your child, otherwise why would you even have created each one with a spirit in the first place? A person has a hard or open heart depending on how they choose to respond to you. However far a person decides to journey into evil is a great offense to you since you made a way to save all people from the destructiveness of evil. A hard heart is hardened against seeing the destructiveness of evil and the love and mercy in you. Your grace is your working in anyone who opens their heart to you. Just because you allowed us to let evil in during earth time doesn't mean that evil is stronger than you in any way. You still have supreme power in the universe. It is not like yin and yang. You did not need evil to give you a balance of power in the universe. You already knew the destructiveness of evil. You already knew that you were completely supreme over evil and that you would easily know how to defeat it, though it would give you sacrificial love pain to do it. You allowed evil to come in just so that your sentient angel and human friends would be able to really choose you.

Romans 9:17–24: "For the Scripture saith unto Pharaoh, 'Even for this same purpose have I raised thee up, that I might shew my power in thee, and that my name might be declared throughout all the earth. Therefore hath he mercy on whom he will have mercy, and whom he will he hardeneth.' Thou wilt say then unto me, 'Why doth he yet find fault? For who hath resisted his will?' Nay but, O man, who art thou that repliest against God? Shall the thing formed say to him that formed, 'Why hast thou made me thus?' Hath not the potter power over the clay, of the same lump to make one vessel unto honour, and another unto dishonour? What if God, willing to shew his wrath, and to make his power known, endured with much longsuffering the vessels of wrath fitted to destruction; and that he might make known the riches of his glory on the vessels of mercy, which he had afore prepared unto glory, Even us, whom he hath called, not of the Jews only, but also of the Gentiles?"

Another oxymoron in the Scriptures seems to be the way you use the word "hate."

Romans 9:10–14: "And not only this; but when Rebecca also had conceived by one, even by our father Isaac; for the children being not yet born, neither having done any good or evil, that the purpose of God according to election might stand, not of works but of him that calleth; it was said unto her, 'The elder shall serve the younger.' As it is written, 'Jacob have I loved, but Esau have I hated.' What shall we say then? Is there unrighteousness with God? God forbid."

Genesis 36:6–7: "And Esau took his wives, and his sons, and his daughters, and all the persons of his house, and his cattle, and all his beasts, and all his substance, which he had got in the land of Canaan; and went into the country from the face of his brother Jacob For their riches were more than that they might dwell together; and the land wherein they were strangers could not bear them because of their cattle."

It certainly doesn't seem like you hated Esau since he had so many blessings given to him in this lifetime. I think when you say you loved Jacob and hated Esau you meant that you called Jacob for a special purpose that you did not choose Esau for. That special purpose was to raise up the Hebrew nation to be a living example in word and deed as a nation to point all the nations to who you, the true God, were, are, and will be. I think when your Bible talks about your election and love and hate like this that you are talking about special calls you put upon some of your children for special purposes. It has nothing to do with calling some for heaven and some for hell, your will is that all humans join you in heaven, and this stays a free choice for them until the day that their body dies.

Luke 14:26: "If any man come to me, and hate not his father, and mother, and wife, and children, and brethren, and sisters, yea, and his own life also, he cannot be my disciple."

Since you talk about loving you, others, and ourselves with your love as your greatest commandment, I know that hate in this verse cannot mean hate the way that we think about hate. I think you are just saying that if our love for you is not greater than we have for anyone or anything else, we will not move forward with you in our friendship. When we come to you in repentance and faith, we need to count this cost that we are recognizing that coming to you means that we desire to put you and your will and our growing relationship with you above anyone or anything else, even our own desires. I think the realization of this is what keeps many people from coming to you and realizing their heart's one true desire.

Exodus 20:3: "Thou shalt have no other gods before me."

Dear God,

You and the Bible are impossible to understand for us humans if we don't have the link from your Spirit to ours.

First Corinthians 2:11–12: "For what man knoweth the things of a man, save the spirit of man which is in him? Even so the things of God knoweth no man, but the Spirit of God. Now we have received, not the spirit of the world, but the spirit which is of God; that we might know the things that are freely given to us of God."

Dear God,
Thank you for reaching out to us to make us your friends throughout all earth time. I want to try to obey your laws because you give them to me as a way to protect against the hurtful consequences that evil always produces. I know you are happy when I try to do your will, but unhappy when I think keeping your laws can earn me things that only you can give me and that I cannot give myself. Your laws show me that there is no way that I can be morally good enough to free myself from evil, only you have the power to wash my sins away. Thank you for doing that. All humans, except Jesus, break your moral laws, but you never disown us or stop working to heal all the hurts in us that evil has caused and still causes.

You don't like divorce any more than you liked a man being married to more than one woman, but you still loved the parents involved in this and you still loved the children of these parents. You keep healing and restoring all the hurts that these things can cause.

Dear God,
Why are you hiding?

Dear Christie,
I am hiding so that you will find me and I will find you. You found me and I found you. Nothing can ever separate you from my love. I made you real in my love and you will never be unreal again. Someday you will know of the joy of living in love with me free from all evil. Until than I will continuously work to restore and heal all the broken pieces of your spirit, soul, and body. While you are on earth, I am allowing evil to exert some of its hurtful consequences, but none of these can ever take you away from being my daughter and eventually being free from evil and all its consequences when you come home to me. Trust me to bring you through your earthly journey, even when you don't understand. When you are frightened, come to me into a different dimension where our garden of love is. Soon we will all be together in this garden in every dimension.

Acts 26:18–24: "To open their eyes, and to turn them from darkness to light, and from the power of Satan unto God, that they may receive forgiveness of sins, and inheritance among them which are sanctified by faith that is in me. And as he thus spake for himself, Festus said with a loud voice, 'Paul, thou are beside thyself; much learning doth make thee mad.'"

Ephesians 3:14–21: "For this cause I bow my knees unto the Father of our Lord Jesus Christ, of whom the whole family in heaven and earth is named. That he would grant you, according to the riches of his glory, to be strengthened with might by his Spirit in the inner man; that Christ may dwell in your hearts by faith; that ye, being rooted and grounded in love may be able to comprehend with all saints what is the breadth, and length, and depth, and height; and to know the love of Christ, which passes knowledge, that ye might be filled with all the fulness of God. Now unto him that is able to do exceeding abundantly above all that we ask or think, according to the power that worketh in us, unto him be glory in the church by Christ Jesus throughout all ages, world without end. Amen."

Dear God,
I think another thing that seems like a contradiction in your Bible is that people feel they need to work their way to heaven by how some verses are written and then other verses seem to say that it is impossible for any human to be good enough to work his or her way to heaven. That is the whole reason that Jesus had to turn himself into a human and die a sacrificial death so any human could receive Jesus' payment for their sin and never have to enter hell to pay for their own sin, but have eternal life with you in heaven. Your differing and nondiffering laws were given to people throughout time to show them what you considered good and evil and that no one could ever keep from doing evil. This would make them realize that they need to put their trust in you to overcome evil for them. Once we are your child, we will want to let you do good through us and our desires to do evil will dim as we see the destructiveness that evil brings. I think even your true children who came to you in repentance and faith and a desire to follow you and received Jesus' gift of salvation, but believe that they have to work to keep their salvation by keeping Bible and church laws, are still your true children, but they will always let in an element of fear into their relationship with you until they really get that you wouldn't have died and rose again if there was any other way for people to gain eternal life. Eternal life is not something we can earn and it is a gift that we receive. We obey you because of our heart, of love for you, not because we will earn our salvation through this obedience. We obey you by listening to your Spirit's voice in our soul before we listen to any other voice.

Chapter Six

Human Consciousness Is Human Spirit and Soul

Dear God,
I came to the beach all by myself. I came into the water to swim despite warnings of strong currents and an ominous-looking sky. Now I am spinning in a current and I don't know down from up. I call to you, Jesus, to help me. You reach for my hand and pull me toward the shore. I take deep breaths as I feel the hard sand and seashells underneath me. I climb away from the tumbling waves, toward the soft sand, and I wake up.

I have been disturbing Barry's sleep since he became disabled, and so I have been sleeping in the spare bedroom. Barry never minds if I crawl in and cuddle with him when I have a nightmare. So I go to Barry's room and flick on the light.

I say, "Barry, honey, I just had a nightmare. May I crawl in with you and cuddle for a while?"

I wait to hear his loving voice say, "Sure, honey."

I don't hear anything. His bed is empty. Where is he? Then I remember that he just died a few weeks ago. Is this still a nightmare. No, this is real. My best friend of forty-two years is gone.

Dear Christie,
He is not gone. He is with me.

Second Corinthians 5:8: "We are confident, I say, and willing rather to be absent from the body, and to be present with the Lord."

Matthew 22:31–32: "But as to touching the resurrection of the dead, have ye not read that which was spoken unto you by God, saying, 'I am the God of Abraham, and the God of Isaac, and the God of Jacob?' God is not the God of the dead, but of the living."

Dear God,
I am glad he is with you. He was suffering so much the last month. All his organs were shutting down and the hospital had to move him to a Hospice Unit to give him comfort in his transition. I know we don't get our new bodies until the rapture, so his soul and spirit do not have a body right now, but I guess he can shape-shift like the angels do if he wants, even though I know we never become angels.

Dear Christie,
What is going on?

Dear God,
I've got painful shingles from stress and I feel so less than perfect because I haven't been trusting you like I should. I feel like I am lost and being torn apart. I don't know if people have bodies when their soul and spirit enters hell at the final judgment, but I know you long for no one to feel the burning pain and thirst of hell. These shingles make me feel what it will be like until your grace burns people away after they have served their punishment and are completely burned away and gone forever because they never became real in your love. Offering free choice for a human to connect or not connect with you forced you to handle the evil in this way for any angels or humans that do not want to connect with you. You have to do this because you are just and good, but your love longs for no one to perish.

Dear Christie,
I am working. When Adam let evil into my world and death entered the world, I already had a plan to completely extinguish evil from my universe without taking away the free choice of angels and humans to choose or not choose me. No human could ever be good enough to stop the destruction of evil, and Barry reached for me in repentance and faith and let me conquer the destructiveness of evil in his spirit and soul and save him for eternal life.

Dear God,

He is your child, but he struggled so to follow you when he was on the earth.

Dear Christie,

Once a human is my child, they are my forever child, and they never stop being my child, even if they choose to remain my baby child during all of their earthly life. They may not experience the joys of greater union with me on earth, but they will experience this in heaven. Barry has this with me now. He has the love, joy, and healing that he always longed to have while he was on earth. He is complete in my love. When people die, their spirit and soul comes to our home where there is love and joy like no one can know on the earth. It is just that those of my children who are still on the earth and choose to not surrender much to my leadings will miss so much. They will miss hearing my voice and direction and feeling my love and friendship, and they will miss some of the awesome ways they could have partnered with me in my fight against evil while they are on the earth. When they die and enter our home, they will have all of that and more with me.

Dear God,

I wish I could come home with you right now. You would be there completely close with me in every way. There would be no pull of evil. Angels and humans would all be close and loving friends. Barry and I would be best friends without hurting each other in any of the ways we did while we were on earth. I long to go home with you. I'm afraid here.

Dear Christie,

I love you. I am invisible to your five senses, but I am not invisible to your consciousness while you are on the earth. Your human consciousness is your soul and spirit. Yes, your body is slated to die and be gone. But your soul and spirit will live forever linked to me and someday every one of my human children will complete their final stage of human metamorphosis and receive an eternal body just like Jesus has now. He is the only human that has completed the final stage of human metamorphosis, even though he is also God. My human children will never be God like Jesus, but they will someday begin eternity complete. I am working to completely overcome evil with good in each of my human children and in the earth and in the universe. I am working and only I know how long. Your soul and spirit will no longer feel the deceitful pull of evil when you come to me, but I am with you and I am stronger than evil even while you are on the earth. I understand why you are afraid on the earth because evil is painful and frightening, but never forget to trust and follow me through your fear, because I am stronger than anyone or anything, especially evil. I know everything. I am all powerful. I am eternal.

Dear God,
I am afraid to write this, my book, because I know I am not getting everything right.

Dear Christie,
I am a part of each person's human life story, or book if you will. I picked the nuclear family first. Then I picked prophets, political leaders, priests, preachers, warriors, teachers, laws, traditions, Israel, the church, apostles, disciples, and others. However, each human has a spirit. Even though their spirit has not yet been made alive in me, they can hear my Spirit calling into their soul and spirit to become my child. I made people a certain way. They have reasoning abilities and a moral conscience. People can never truly become alive unless they surrender to me and become my child through repentance and faith. They were never designed to be real apart from me.

Dear God,
I am joined with you as your child, but I still get so many things confused and wrong as I live out my days on the earth.

Dear Christie,
That is called being human. Humans can never be God. Humans will have to fight the pull of sin on the earth until the day they die. I work through humans to help other humans see more truths about me, but no human can ever completely get it all right on this earth. As long as a human gets the main truth right that they need to come to me in repentance and faith with a willingness to follow me to become my child, then they can enter eternity with me and have a real life linked to mine. Jesus is the only way. Humans have always needed to come to me to be made mine through repentance and faith, and Jesus conquered evil for everyone. Even though people may not have entirely understood how I would work through my Messiah before Jesus died, they need to believe that Jesus was and is my Messiah after he died. All people need to do is believe that I am the one true God and come to me in repentance and faith, and they are my forever child. All the sins of a person are forgiven for a human as soon as they become my child, but if they want me to help them with the hurt that sin inflicts on the earth, they need to experience my grace, which is them allowing me to work

in them, after salvation, so that they can experience intimacy with me on the earth, as well as in heaven.

Dear God,
It is easier for me to notice the sins in others than in myself, but you ask me to let you deal with sin your way in myself, first of all, and only get involved instructing others about what sins they are involved in under your loving guidance. I have so often been harsh with others and myself instead of forgiving and praying for others and myself. Love extinguishes evil much more than human anger.

Dear Christie,
You have to continually be forgiving yourself and others and surrender to my guidance on how to deal with everyone and everything. You are not alone. You have me. Receive my grace instead of getting smashed up by guilt and shame. Grace is for salvation and then you will come to heaven no matter what, but grace is also for after salvation to help you see things more from my point of view, especially your identity, the identity of others, and my true character and identity.

Dear God,
At Barry's funeral, both Ricky and Ryan commented how Barry made them feel provided for and protected. He did that for me too. Thank you for giving him to Ricky, Ryan, and me. We miss him. I wouldn't call him back here to this world though because I know he is finally feeling the deep love that he was always wanting to feel on this earth and never quite felt. I know you are healing him emotionally and spiritually and physically, and he is out of pain. I'm glad he is with you. Like Ricky said, he was a wonderful singer and he may have always wanted to have his music go further than it did, but he did something even more wonderful, he put a song in the heart of everyone he loved. I guess your love trumps everything and I can completely trust you because you are love.

Dear Christie,
I placed you on the earth at this time for a reason. I have good paths for you to travel. All people are individuals and you are an individual. I don't make you less of who you are when I synergistically blend my Spirit with yours—I make you more who you are, the person you really know I made you to be inside, the person that you really want to be. You need to understand me in a way when I don't do everything your way because I have an individual life story and plan, a book if you will, for each person. We are

writing the book of your life together. I know what is best for each person. I am what is best for each person. I want to partner with you as you live your life. I know when each person will be born and I know when each person will die. All good gifts that come to people come from me. What appear to be circumstances or coincidences are often my interventions in human life, especially when prayer, trust, and obedience are involved. I put all the puzzle pieces of life together in amazing ways and someday the puzzle will be complete. Remember the love and help that you and Barry brought to each other and let the rest go, because I do. That is what redemption is all about. Remember the blessings that came into your life when you followed my ways. The world may make good look like evil and evil look like good, but I know what is evil and what is good. Evil hurts and love heals. I love you. You are my precious daughter. Hold onto my hand and trust me. My words in the Bible and in your heart are a light onto your path. It is okay that you are not perfect because I love you perfectly and I make all things work together for good, even things that are not good. I love you.

Dear God,
Death became real to me when it reached into my personal little world and took someone that my life revolved around. Now that it is here, Barry is just so gone. I don't hear him in my consciousness like when we were separated. He is in a different world from me and I cannot access him. I wouldn't call him back to the pain and suffering of this world and I know your love is healing him completely on every level. There is nothing better than being completely home with you. I feel alone until I remember that you are always with me.

Jesus was here and gone but we can still access him by way of our spirit and soul being connected to his spirit and soul. You call into every human heart, to their soul and spirit, to their consciousness that you created—you long for each one to become truly yours.

I want so much to grow closer and closer to you. I hope this prayer journal stirs the desire of many humans to want to become your child. If they are your child I hope it stirs a desire in them to want to grow closer and closer in intimacy with you.

You knew that humans could have lived forever on the earth if they hadn't let evil in. Since you knew they would let evil in, you had a plan for their body to die and to bring the soul and spirit to you to escape the second death for every human who chose to connect with you, and someday you will give them a new body. You knew what you had to do to have sentient beings who could eternally share your love as your family and friends, and you did it.

While evil is allowed on the earth, you allow fallen and unfallen angels, believing and unbelieving humans, to view the interplay and consequences of good and evil on the earth so that those who choose to be yours will really understand experientially why you hate evil the way you do. You allow us synergistically to partner with you to fight evil and shine a light on who you, the true God, are ,and what you want with us so that we will all understand even more about your character and heart. I'll stop thinking that maybe you should have set things up differently than you did, because I am not God and you are, and I completely trust that you know what you are doing in overcoming evil with your goodness and love. I'll stop blaming you when evil touches me, because it never comes from you and only you know why you do not stop it right away, but you will stop it all eventually in your perfect timing. If you were not here, evil would never end because only you have the power and wisdom to end it without becoming evil yourself. You have to bring punishment because you are just, but your grace will have an end to the punishment. I will never completely understand you and your ways, but I'm glad I have eternity to understand more and more about you and draw closer and closer into your love and friendship. Why are you hiding while we are on this earth? I can hardly wait until you are no longer hiding when I am with you in our home in heaven and there will be no blocks to our shared love.

Dear Christie,
When I first made people, I visited with them every day bodily. When they let in evil, I did start hiding completely in the spirit realm except for the times Jesus made his bodily appearances, but any human has always been able to find me. I hide, but I call into the consciousness or soul and spirit of each human to find me with their soul and spirit and become mine through deciding to follow me because they realize that I am who I am. I will help anyone find me and become mine who honestly seeks me and wants me. Even after a human is mine and they can access my Spirit with their spirit, I am still hiding in the spiritual relm and I can be blocked or unblocked depending on how intimate they want to get with me in surrendering their will to mine. Their greatest internal happiness and fulfillment will be the times they willingly surrender to my will. I never bring evil. I am fighting evil. I lament the damage that evil does to people. You will just have to trust me and understand, even though you don't understand, that your faith in me is my plan for you on this earth, and it is the best plan to overcome evil with good while obtaining true believing children, and helping everyone understand what good and evil and hate and love really are. You will have to not be angry with me when evil touches you, but realize

that I am using it and defusing it in my own time and in my own way. I am overcoming evil with love.

Dear God,
Thank you for patiently talking all these things out with me. I believe in you. I believe your Bible is all true and the thoughts you give to me that I can discern are all true. I love you. Thank you for loving me.

Made in the USA
Columbia, SC
05 October 2021